PRAISE FOR *MAKING YOUR FIRS*

"*Making Your First Blockbuster* is a must-read for an ....ucing or directing anything, and I wish I'd had it at hand from my earliest student-film days. With clarity and a passion for excellence, Paul Dudbridge demystifies some of the most challenging aspects of film storytelling, covering everything from script and character development to making explosions look real. If you read this book and absorb its lessons, you can show up on set with confidence and lead your crew to blockbuster success."
—**Christopher Vogler**, author, worldwide bestseller *The Writer's Journey*

"We've all been taught that low-budget movies should be simple and unambitious, a couple of people talking around a table. Paul Dudbridge explodes this myth and goes on to explain how you can put the action and excitement from your favorite films into your own work. Step by step, with plenty of examples, he breaks down everything: script, cinematography, special effects, picture, and sound editing. At every stage, invaluable advice is offered on how to make your movie as rich and cinematic as possible. I wish I had had this book when I first started out!"
—**Neil Oseman**, Director of Photography, *The Little Mermaid*, *Heretiks*, *Ren: The Girl with the Mark*

"An insightful, intelligent, and thoroughly entertaining introduction to filmmaking on both a modest and larger scale. Packed with well-chosen examples and anecdotes, it gently takes your hand and guides you through the labyrinth process of movie creation with awareness, technical savvy, and humor."
—**Michael Riley**, feature film producer, *Crowhurst*, *Chosen*, *The Seasoning House*

"A superb book, useful for both experienced filmmakers and novices. A highly informative insiders' guide to the entire moviemaking process."
—**Manuel Puro**, casting director, *Moon*, *Mute*, *The Machine*

"A comprehensive, jargon-free, bullsh*t-busting guide to everything you need to know. Leaving you no excuses to get out there and make that feature film."
—**Tom Brereton Downs**, screenology.com (production company, film school, movement)

"*Making Your First Blockbuster* hits all the important approaches and insights on working with stunts. Not just the safety aspects, but how to best shoot action for the screen and work collaboratively with the stunt team."
—**Neil Chapelhow**, stuntman, *Wonder Woman, Solo: A Star Wars Story, Justice League*

"This aspirational guide covers many of the creative / technical processes for narrative filmmaking. Dudbridge has a clear passion for storytelling, profession-alism, and the spectacular. This exciting book includes inspirational quotes and practical advice. A fantastic addition for emerging filmmakers with sights set on making the next big blockbuster!"
—**Dr. Allister Gall**, cofounder, Imperfect Cinema and Film; TV lecturer at Plymouth University

MAKING YOUR FIRST
BLOCKBUSTER
WRITE IT, FILM IT, BLOW IT UP!

PAUL DUDBRIDGE

MICHAEL WIESE PRODUCTIONS

Published by Michael Wiese Productions
12400 Ventura Blvd. #1111
Studio City, CA 91604
(818) 379-8799, (818) 986-3408 (FAX)
mw@mwp.com
www.mwp.com

Cover design by Johnny Ink. www.johnnyink.com
Interior design by William Morosi
Copyediting by Ross Plotkin
Printed by McNaughton & Gunn

Library of Congress Cataloging-in-Publication Data

Names: Dudbridge, Paul, 1977- author.
Title: Making your first blockbuster : write it, film it, blow it up! / Paul Dudbridge.
Description: Studio City, CA : Michael Wiese Productions, [2019]
Identifiers: LCCN 2018027813 | ISBN 9781615932962
Subjects: LCSH: Blockbusters (Motion pictures)--Production and direction.
Classification: LCC PN1995.9.B598 D83 2019 | DDC 791.4302/32--dc23
LC record available at https://lccn.loc.gov/2018027813

Printed on Recycled Stock

Dedicated to my parents, Margaret and Ken.
My mom for introducing me to many a blockbuster in my younger years, and my Dad for letting me steal the family's video camera when I was 11 to shoot my first movie. Between the two, my future was sealed.

TABLE OF CONTENTS

ACKNOWLEDGMENTS

This book wouldn't have been possible without the kind help and cooperation of a number of important people.

My actors / models: Mhairi Calvey, Simon Pengelly, Steve Aaron-Sipple, Alicia Ancel-Browne. Alan Tabrett for all your assistance with my graphics and illustrations. Sam Norman for some of my screengrabs and lending me your camera equipment, Simon Pearce for being brilliant and supportive as ever throughout the whole book, Joe Golby and Neil Chapelhow for your expert proofreading skills on the stunts and fight section, Mark Turner at MTFX for assisting with all my special effects pictures, Fiona Francombe at The Bottle Yard Studios, Bristol, for allowing me to use your site for some images, Marc Pearce for allowing me

to use stills from your movie, and Rob Partridge from Perdix Firearms for your help and proofreading skills in making sure the firearms section was all legally and technically correct. Joseph Cruz at the California Film Commission, and Larry Zanoff at Independent Studio Services, for your advice on having firearms on set in the USA. My excellent copy editor, Ross Plotkin, and my designer, Bill Morosi.

Last, but certainly not least, I extend my eternal gratitude to Michael Wiese and Ken Lee at Michael Wiese Productions for allowing me to write a second book for their company. All their support, understanding, and input were much appreciated during the writing and production of *Making Your First Blockbuster*. I thank you.

INTRODUCTION

*"The best advice I could give is to take your work to the
imaginative extreme, as far as you can creatively go. Be dangerous.
If it has enough of your voice and passion in it, others will
see it as original, and it will stand out and get noticed."*
— PEN DENSHAM, WRITER / PRODUCER / DIRECTOR

*You're about to read the book I
wish I had when I was 18.*

Let's start with a script:

INT. LIVING ROOM — DAY

One Saturday afternoon, a
mom sits her seven-year-old
boy down to watch *Raiders
of the Lost Ark*. The
boy is mesmerized as the
swashbuckling hero punches,
swings, and slides his
way through scrape after
scrape. The boulder chases
after Indy, Indy shoots the
swordsman in the market,
Indy rams the Nazi jeep

off the cliff and soldiers
fall hundreds of feet in
the exciting truck chase
through the desert . . .

                  BOY
That's a really big drop,
isn't it? I know it's just
a movie but did they just
let two actors . . . die?
That's not really real, is
it, Mom?

Spectacular, swashbuckling adven-
tures filled with action and special
effects have always captured my
imagination. It's easy to be absorbed
and transported into another world,
swept up by the grandeur and magic

0.1. Indiana Jones chasing bad guys in *Raiders of the Lost Ark* (1981).

of the movies. The same ambition kept rattling around my head: *I want to experience that world. How do I get to play there?*

There was this book in my local library when I was a kid. I used to ride there after school, lock my bike up, and go in and sit down to leaf through its pages time and time again. It was a book about special effects and contained cartoon images breaking down how all those wonderful effects in movies had been done. We saw the director, actor, and camera operator at work, and then the special effects technician off camera sprinkling snow over the actor's heads. Another section showed Superman in front of a large projection screen pretending he was flying. I was hooked.

The 14-year-old me even had my first attempt at special effects when I put some firecrackers inside my Millennium Falcon *Star Wars* toy (please don't tell my parents). It

blew up but didn't look particularly spectacular. The build-up was more exciting than the actual effect, to be honest. I'm sure Industrial Light and Magic (ILM) could have done it a lot better.

As the years went by, my teenage friends and I tried different ways to make our own effects-laden block-buster action films. Firecrackers served as a good replacement to squibs (bullet-hit effects) until I got my hands on the real thing. With the firecrackers cello-taped to the wall nearby, we would roll cameras, light the fuse . . . and *bang!* The action would kick off! We'd cut in just as the firecracker went off, and the effect was complete — somebody was shooting at us!

One event that I still rue could have landed me in a 10' x 8' cell. I was 18, and we'd just wrapped a day of running around some empty ware-house for our action movie, blasting our blank-firing pistols at each other. On the way home, my buddy asked me for gas money. "Sure!" I said. "Pull over and let me go to this ATM." I jumped out, but it was out of order, so I ran into the nearby bank instead. I waited in line and got my cash over the counter before running out and jumping back in the waiting car outside. Then it happened . . . A blank-firing gun, holstered under my jacket and strapped around my chest, fell out and onto the passenger seat. My heart stopped for what felt like an eternity. I had a flash of what might have happened had it fallen out as I ran *into* the bank! How would I explain to the armed police officers, security guards, and judge that although I did want the money in the bank, it was in fact mine, and I wasn't actually robbing the joint? The correct and proper way of using and storing blank-firing firearms will be discussed later.

See how this book would have been useful to me back then?

WHAT WE ARE COVERING IN THIS BOOK

Let's consider how you can make *your* blockbuster be the best it can be, whatever type of film it is. Maybe you're making your big action film, or a comedy, or science-fiction, a western, or a horror film. We're talking

about blockbusters — but my film-making tutorials can be applied to any type of movie. Your full-throttle action picture with bar fights (stunts / action) might feature a finale involving a warehouse shootout (guns / special effects) before the building blows up (visual effects); or . . . you could be making a romantic drama where a character's fiancé tragically dies in a car crash (stunts / action) before she meets the new love of her life, finally kissing him in the rain (special effects). Perhaps they drive off together toward a gorgeous sunset (green screen / visual effects) at the end. The actual writing, shooting, action / stunts, special effects, and visual effects information contained in these pages is equally relevant to quiet dramas, low-budget comedies, or whatever *blockbuster* you are making.

My first aim is to punch up your story, photography, and the mechanics of how your film fits together, addressing any action, stunts, or special effects work that may be required. We'll look at every-thing regarding the creative side of blockbuster moviemaking. How you raise capital, manage the budget, and sell your film is a whole other book. Special or visual effects and stunts might cost you money, neces-sitating professionals — or you might be lucky enough to have everyone you need right at your disposal. Do whatever you need to in your planning and shooting so the final product is the best it can be. No matter how you work these elements in, I'll help you decide what tool is right for the job and how to shoot and edit your movie's final shots. How resourceful you are in acquiring special effects technicians, visual effects artists, or stunt crews is up to you. These technicians are seldom as far away as you might think. For my first action film, I wanted to end on a huge fireball explosion. I rang a local theatrical lighting company for advice, and they referred me to a special effects technician who was just starting out. I called him and he offered to do my effect for a fraction of the cost he would charge big productions. This was over 25 years ago, too, long before Google allowed one to easily find people online. It's time to get resourceful . . .

In my first book, *Shooting Better Movies: The Student Filmmakers' Guide*, I covered all the technical aspects of the camera from the aperture, depth of field, shutter, and so forth. You need an understanding of these areas, or I'll be spending the first half repeating myself. Or, of course, go buy my first book. Since this book is aimed at the intermediate-level / professional filmmaker, I'll assume you know a fair bit already about film's technical components and shooting logistics. I will do a little recap for

those in need, but then comes the more intricate, exciting stuff — try and keep up!

I want to ensure your blockbuster looks and sounds like it should. Raise your standards so your image and soundscape are the highest quality they can be. Having worked with lots of students over the years and seen hundreds of low-budget films, I regularly see overexposed actors, jerky camera pans, out-of-focus shots, and dodgy edits, and hear off-mic and dropped-out audio. This falls short of blockbuster standards. Or I see the exact opposite: gorgeous photography, amazing visual effects, stunning soundscape, but no indication of plot or an engaging story. We will look a little bit at story — and scriptwriting, cinematography, directing, and post-production sound techniques — to really make your blockbuster shine. You can have the best choreographed fight in the history of cinema, but if it's poorly shot or badly edited, it's not gonna sell. You're aiming to cast the right actor, who speaks the well-written dialogue, all lit and composed in the perfect frame to tell the captivating story. You also need the scene to be tightly cut and supported by an awesome sound mix. I want to pack as many hints, tips, suggestions, and techniques as I can into each area so your "blockbuster" has a massive opening weekend!

0.2. A bold new way of blockbuster moviemaking arrived with *Star Wars* (1977).

SO WHAT IS A BLOCKBUSTER?

First, a little history. Perhaps the first "blockbuster" dates from way back in 1939: the epic *Gone With the Wind*. Audiences flocked to the theaters in droves to see this movie set during the American Civil War. They subsequently rereleased it in theaters for years after so audiences could enjoy it over and over again. It wasn't until the 1970s that we saw the blockbuster really arrive on our screens, though. Steven Spielberg's *Jaws* (1975) was the first film to screen in over 100 theaters, and it changed the way movies would be released forever. It became a phenomenon and the first film to top $100,000,000 at the box office. Two years later it would happen again, but on an even grander scale. George Lucas's *Star Wars* (1977) changed everything. With its state-of-the-art special effects, worn and dirty worlds, and rough, ready characters, it offered a bold new way of moviemaking. The frame was layered and filled with excitement as space-ships whizzed by camera chased by enemy cruisers blasting laser beams. It was spectacular in its epic score, sweeping landscapes, and vast array of planets and robots. Then there was the merchandising: the T-shirts, soundtracks, coffee mugs, and, later, the toy figures and games. With the release of the merchandising, you got to own a piece of the movie by owning a character — even if it was only 3½ inches tall.

Since then, we've had our fair share of blockbusters every year. Some hit big like *Jurassic Park* (1993), *Titanic* (1997), and *Furious 7* (2015), and some fall short like *The Last Action Hero* (1993), *John Carter* (2012), or *King Arthur: Legend of the Sword* (2017). There is no proven formula to these things; it's just what audiences are looking for at a given time. Critically, blockbusters haven't fared too well; sometimes this affects the box office, and sometimes it makes no difference at all. *Transformers* (2007) and its subsequent sequels have been critically panned but made a fortune at the box office. *Blade Runner 2049* (2017) was critically applauded but bombed with ticket buyers. Sometimes, everything aligns and you get a film like *Wonder Woman* (2017), which did good box office and found a place in critics' hearts. Blockbusters can be financially and critically successful if they arrive at just the right time. Other examples could be *Gladiator* (2000), the *Lord of the Rings* trilogy (2001–2003), *The Dark Knight* (2008), *The Avengers* (2012), or *Inception* (2010), all well received financially and critically. Repeat viewings often yield big box office returns too; people return to theaters to see a movie over and over again, and producers know they have a big hit on their hands.

Sometimes blockbusters don't get the respect they deserve. With the story being slightly higher concept or fantastical makes people or reviewers equate it with subpar characterization and quality. It can't possibly be any good with a story about aliens or robots at its core, can it? Good storytelling, acting, characterization, and technical prowess are not reserved

for serious dramatic stories and are not mutually exclusive. You can of course have superheroes, explosions, and comic-book stories containing these positive attributes too. Look at James Mangold's *Logan* (2017), which was even nominated for Best Adapted Screenplay at the 2018 Oscars. In addition, the near-military operation required to coordinate and execute movies of this type and scale is immense. It's easy to see why blockbuster movies get a bad rap, though. Occasionally, we are treated to stereotypical, thinly drawn characters who throw tanks at each other in a heavy CGI-laden finale until the city collapses! Much of the public learns about the film because of its large marketing budget and hype machine. But even the serious independent drama can suffer from poor creative choices, albeit a little less colorfully and with less noise and visual trickery. Yet sometimes the revenue earned by tent-pole blockbusters enable their studios or production companies to take chances on smaller, more independent films that otherwise might not have seen the light of day. They can afford to make these quirkier, more intimate films due to the returns from the larger, mainstream blockbusters. Everything has its place.

Maybe your blockbuster is an epic, spectacular, effects-laden masterpiece costing thousands or even millions of dollars, or maybe it's being shot in your parents' front room for hundreds. Either way, I can't tell you how to fund your blockbuster. I can tell you how to make it the best it can be. Let's get your movie as close as possible to what you see at the theater by using some inspired writing techniques, intricate cinematography approaches, and helpful directing and editing tips. *Let's get the script right and the edit tight!*

So buckle up. I'm about to throw a lot of information at you that will hopefully make your blockbuster movie a smash at the box office.

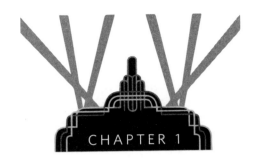

CHAPTER 1

WRITING YOUR BLOCKBUSTER

*"There was a time when the action movie was
character based, not spectacle based."*
— JAMES MANGOLD, DIRECTOR

It all starts with the script. You may have heard stories about how some blockbusters have a release date and no script, but start shooting nonetheless, and end up with problems. Let's not go down that road . . . In this chapter, I want to talk about the story points, tips, and ideas that can make your script impossible to put down. I won't be talking too much about formats or layout, as that can be found in a host of other books. Instead I'll use some examples from my own work and recent blockbusters to discuss interesting elements designed to make your script irresistible.

THE WRITING PROCESS

Everyone's process is different. Some do months or years of research before touching a keyboard or putting pen to paper; others just start and find their way as they go. Find the method that works for you. I write out the story in note form first. This could be single lines, paragraphs, or just a random splurge of ideas that gets rearranged and taken apart. Off that, I expand each line or paragraph into scenes, and after a little more evolution I find the structure. I now have a treatment of about 10 pages. It is then that I send it out to writer friends for feedback; after I have their notes, I start the actual script. Feedback given about your treatment is important; some setups and certain character traits need to be woven into the story from the beginning, and it's best to lock this stuff down early rather than waiting until the script is done. Issues will be ironed out in the rewrite, but important details that impact the story should be pinned down at the beginning. This works for me, as I know the story plays well, and the structure is properly sequenced. How I will actually write it comes on the day, but I know I'm not wasting my time when I begin.

I used to start with no game plan; the story and characters existed only in my head. My old method caused trouble with setups and payoffs. I had to go back and shoehorn in objects or character traits to make my ending work. After a while not knowing where the story was going, I pondered: *What should I do now?* This lack of direction soon resulted in boredom and self-doubt. I began to worry: *Should I pack it in?* Maybe you've been here yourself. How many writers have unfinished scripts? The hard work lies in blocking out the structure, enabling the actual scriptwriting process to be a wonderful and enjoyable experience. All I'm then thinking about in that moment is the dialogue. The characters and plot have all be taken care of, otherwise when you sit down to write, you're juggling character, story, structure, dialogue, and poetic stage directions all at once. You're bound to drop one.

So what can we draw up to help us prepare for writing the script? You don't have to do everything listed below, but using some of these may benefit you.

Logline — A short, one- or two-line sentence that tells the story. Good to have ready if people ask what your script is about, and handy for selling packages if you're trying to get your work financed. A logline is designed to sell a film by piquing public interest, and is not to be confused with a poster tagline, something very different. Here are some logline examples:

"When a desperate father needs money to fund his dying daughter's operation, he hatches a plan to rob a bank run by his father-in-law."

"An American comes to the U.K. to search for a son he never knew existed, only to get caught up in an underground organ-trafficking ring."

Outline — The whole story laid out and used for your writing purposes only. Not who the characters are or what they say, just your story points. This can be as long as you need, but probably about 3 or 4 pages.

Beat sheet — A scene-by-scene breakdown with a line of description for each, allowing the story and structure layout to be seen at a glance. It's quickly evident in this form with no need to wade through paragraphs of text if a story point is happening too early or too late.

The 1-pager — The long synopsis takes us through the setup, protagonist, antagonist, and ending. There's a good chance others will see this, so make it good. If you need a 1-pager for sales purposes and didn't prepare one initially, use your finished script to draw something up. It could be an edited version of the treatment, jazzed up to make it sell.

Treatment — A document you circulate detailing your film's whole story. If you're asked by a producer or agent to submit a treatment for your script, you have one ready. Treatments are about 10 pages long and sometimes contain a little dialogue. The entire story, including the ending, gets told; treatments aren't meant to lure readers to a mysterious finale by asking questions or creating suspense. Make the treatment as exciting as it can be, as this is the document a studio head's assistant, agent, or investor might be reading. These people are busy; get your story across to them in an exciting way, one that really sings.

I've picked up hundreds of tips and pieces of advice from books and blogs about writing. They might address story mechanics, the writing process, or script development. One pearl of wisdom in William Goldman's *Which Lie Did I Tell?* is about just getting something down on the page. Goldman was visiting a theater director in New York who was working on a dance show. The director looked up from his conversation to see the performers had stopped dancing. After inquiring why, the reply came back. "That's all we got. We don't know what to do next."

The director replied, "Have them do *something*. Anything. Then we have something to change . . ." That stuck with me and has worked in my favor on many different levels. From writing scripts to editing films to writing this book! Just put something down. It doesn't have to be perfect, so long as we can tell if it's working. Seeing what doesn't work sometimes gives us an idea of what will. It is then that we can see the story really beginning to take shape.

STORY AND STRUCTURE

Story is the most important thing. If a film doesn't work, is boring, or fails to grab your attention in any way, these problems probably come from issues with story. Sometimes trailers have spectacular visuals, a big star, and that awesome stunt, but still leave me a little unimpressed. Here I normally ask, "What's the story?" It can be set up with one line! If it's missing, the audience won't be intrigued and they'll fail to show up at the theater. Someone has gone missing. Who took them, and will they be found? Characters are stuck on an island / space station / underground. Will they escape? Who will survive? A question is asked, and the audience needs it answered.

Here's the best tip when thinking about story: Start as late as you possibly can. When does the story really begin? Just before things kick off, before any life-changing incidents take place, we need to see our hero in their ordinary world. Any earlier, we might question if the information being given has any relevance to the story about to unfold.

What is the difference between story and plot? Think of story as the emotional journey the characters make, with plot being the physical journey. Telling someone your story gives a sense of mood, feel, and character. Telling someone the plot of your film is to tell them what happens from A to B to C. Viewers are moved by the story, not the plot. Characters need to go on both a physical and an emotional journey. Some films, according to their genre, will have more of one than the other. If an

action film is criticized for being soulless, then perhaps it has all physical journey and not much of an emotional one. Good stories, essentially, are about character.

A subplot can also be interwoven throughout the main story. It may be a love story of sorts: a romantic entanglement or some kind of relationship drama that centers on matters of the heart. The subplot is useful, giving you something to cut to from the main story; it works best when it relates to the main plot and central theme of the film. Eventually the subplot meets up with the main plot, and you can resolve both.

Each of these story beats needs to be organized and positioned to get the best out of it. This positioning is called structure. Structure is akin to a steel rod down the back of a clay sculpture. It is never seen or touched by the audience, but if you took it away, the sculpture would fall apart. The hardest job for the writer is positioning these beats. Each one affects the tone and pace, and determines what information is released to the audience and when. Traditionally we have a three-act structure — beginning, middle, and end — with major beats happening on the act breaks. Three is a nice dramatic number and works very well. It is even possible to have a four- or five-act structure. Or maybe your film is set in real time, or has multiple stories weaved into one film. Structures can vary, but they are usually crucial to a film's pacing. If things happen too early or too late, audiences can feel unsettled, bored, or confused. I have also used index cards to help with structure. You list every scene on small 6" x 4" cards and pin them up so it's immediately obvious where each scene sits. Seeing each scene on cards or written as a single sentence might reveal similar scenes clumped together or lots of exposi-tional story beats happening back to back. Maybe you have four scenes in a row that are all interiors or all exteriors. This might be okay for story purposes, but it might also highlight issues that you've missed. Index cards let you step back and see the beats and structure as a whole, rather than the blinkered view of each individual scene at a time.

For a film to work and be successful, it has to have a good story. It's not the prose in the script or the witty dialogue, or your strict adherence to format, but story. The audience needs to have a well-told and moving tale to help them forget who they are for two hours.

OBSTACLES

Whatever your protagonist wants, a host of obstacles should be littered along their path to prevent or dissuade them from achieving it. Obstacles

come in the shape or form of distance, people, objects, machines, robots, weather, armies, or even society. A host of possibilities await. These obstacles also help create conflict, internal and external, that can add drama to the story.

Conflict and obstacles can be wonderful things to think up and write. Each character has struggles, needs, aspirations, and desires. What can we throw at our characters to keep things interesting on that journey? What would be the worst thing we could do to them to really test their physical ability, and perhaps more importantly, their emotional resil-ience? Sometimes the best conflict is between right and right, not between right and wrong. Maybe there are two options that both have merit. This is when your character is really put to the test. The audience is able to relate to their struggle and then identify with the character.

RESOLUTIONS

How does your story end? It's the resolution of a movie that audiences leave with, so it better be good. The last ten minutes of any film should be unimpeachable, wrapping up all the loose ends sprinkled and set up by the writer. In real life things don't always work out, and bad people don't always get caught or face comeuppance, but movie audiences want to see some sort of justice. You risk losing them if they're not satisfied. The film needn't have a happy ending, but the story has to come to a satisfactory conclusion. Maybe the character has a new outlook or direction in life; they don't get the job but maybe get the girl. *They must get some sort of closure.*

The Clint Eastwood movie *Blood Work* (2002) offered an interesting resolution. An aging cop (Eastwood) is chasing and being tormented by a serial killer. The killer then murders a woman, whose heart is given to Eastwood during a transplant operation. The victim's sister tracks down Eastwood and asks him to find the killer. The audience wants the end of the film to involve Eastwood doing what he does best: finally shooting the killer. But what about the sister? She wants revenge for her sister's murder, surely. So how do director Eastwood and writer Brian Helgeland tie it all up? Well, during the climatic shootout on a boat taking on water, Eastwood shoots and brings down the killer. Dead? Not quite, still breathing . . . until the sister comes along and holds the killer's head down and he drowns. They both played a part in the killer's demise, and the audience got what they were after from each of the characters.

How do we handle the demise of the villain if the hero hasn't killed before or it's simply not in their character? Your accountant or housewife heroine probably shouldn't brandish a machine gun and waste the bad guy if that's not her lifestyle. *The villain's demise has to be at the hero's hand.* Instead of the hero taking a key action (pulling the trigger or pushing the bad guy off the roof) that results in the death of the villain, you may orchestrate the villain about to fall off a roof or get eaten by a monster, and it's the hero's *inaction* that lets it happen. Their lack of action can lead to the demise of the villain, who for moral reasons must die — but now the hero's behavior isn't out of character. It also means they don't have blood on their hands, which might have led to their arrest. They've still had significant involvement in the death of the person responsible, and everyone leaves the theater happy.

SCENE DESCRIPTIONS

Scene descriptions tell the reader what's happening. The reader needs to know character activity, about any important objects, and environmental and visual cues. You should strive to create feeling and imagination in the reader, not just give them a laundry list of descriptions. We know where we are, thanks to the scene heading above; now we need action. Scene descriptions are also an opportunity for the writer to display their voice. Good writing isn't just witty dialogue.

Make it fun for the reader, something beyond a mere blueprint for shooting.

Make your character's actions more than just "walking" or "looking." How do they walk? How do they look? Choosing to use "jogs," "skips," "saunters," "glances," "stares," "ogles," or any other verbs helps convey so much more to the reader and gives us that sense of feeling and a clue to the character's intent. It also helps the actor who has to perform this action.

You don't need to tell us about the wardrobe, the kitchen, or what the set looks like in any detail unless this information is pivotal to the scene. A slight hint sparks the audience to deduce all that other stuff. Let the production designer worry about what everything looks like. Can you find a description that sets the scene and feel, and shows motion and character? If you can achieve at least one of these, you're on your way.

Don't tell us when the incidental music starts or what camera angles are being used; leave these concerns to the composer and director. But if a scene features music that the characters can hear, instructions about it starting, stopping, growing too loud, or in any way affecting the characters *do* need to go in. One possible exception to the "don't write camera angles" rule is if the angle is essential for a scene to make sense. Maybe you have the characters someplace they don't know they are in danger, and the camera

pulls back to reveal the threat. Use it extremely sparingly, if at all.

Choose details in the descriptions that imply other things too. I call it the "tip of the iceberg." The audience reads a small amount and can assume or imagine the rest. Not only do you write less, but you now have the audience engaged and doing the work for you. In his script for the Bruce Willis action film *The Last Boy Scout* (1991), action screenwriter Shane Black describes a car chase simply as: "The cars trade paint." If you can tell a story with your images and then add dialogue to fill in any gaps, you're in a good place.

What do you feel when you turn a page to see a big block of dense text? If you're like me, part of you recoils at the work that lies ahead. It's off-putting for the reader, so break your action into four or five lines. Normally this length fits any singular unit of action quite nicely too. It is the same amount of text, but it looks like less to read. By breaking the action down this way, you're also creating an edit of sorts in the audience's head. A new paragraph / unit of action signifies a new shot, and separates it from the one before.

Some poorly written scripts even put character backstory in scene descriptions. This won't translate to the screen. "Marc, 40s, tall, smiling, though his eyes hide a lot of pain and years of abuse" doesn't travel past the page. Years of pain and abuse cannot simply be shot, nor will the audience understand it just because you wrote it in the character's introduction. Find another way of getting that information across. *The reader knows the information, but the film audience will not.* This contradictory description *could* give an actor a rough idea of character, but is ill-suited to convey plot.

DIALOGUE

The dialogue has to ring true for the character and situation, and should therefore be want-driven. Once you know your character and their backstory, the dialogue you craft will become more authentic. The characters will eventually write their own dialogue; then you're on your way. I've had this moment and discussed it with other writers; it is strange and amazing. You can't write fast enough to get the lines down! Pages can spill out at breakneck speed and make the writing experience great fun.

If I find myself a little fuzzy and I don't know just yet what to have the characters say to each other, I just have them talk rubbish until they find the thread themselves. After about three or four lines, the true nature of the scene will come out. Then I just cut the opening rubbish that got me to that place. Remember the William

Goldman story: *Put something down, then you have something to change.*

Movies have movie dialogue, not real dialogue. If everything in a movie was "real," we would have every character "ummm-ing" and "arrr-ing" every couple of lines. Movies are wish fulfilment; people say the right thing at the right time. Don't be afraid of writing this; the audience wants it. Characters' intentions generally come out during performance, but writers give voice to those characters' thoughts. You may have moments in the script where characters say stuff they simply don't need to; their expression will say it all. Film is a visual medium; if a story can be told in pictures, all the better. Cut dialogue to its bare minimum and look for ways to tell your story visually.

This is also the time to add subtext to the mix. Sub, meaning "beneath." So what is going on beneath the text? What is the scene really about? Not necessarily what it appears to be about. Subtext can be dialogue that goes against the nature of the scene being played out. Subtext is revealed through both character positioning and action. If their actions visually contradict their dialogue, you're communicating a different message. Subtext can come across through connotations or associated meanings of words spoken; they will have two meanings, one direct and one less so, because of the context surrounding your scene.

CHARACTERS

Cars can crash and roll down the street and alien ships can blow up a building, but if there isn't a character inside that we care about, it's all moot. A three-dimensional interesting character helps actors and makes for entertaining viewing. Action films sometimes get accused of having very thin, stereotypical characters, selling tickets instead through special effects and spectacle. This may be true sometimes, but it's quite possible to have both.

So how do you create interesting characters? How do we write characters that are complex and multifaceted? Start by jotting down a small breakdown of each one. What are their likes and dislikes? What was their upbringing like? Relationships, religious beliefs, parents, skills, hobbies, attitudes, morals, values, flaws, fears, secrets, traits . . . Then a paragraph summing them up. Backstory work adds layers to the story and creates more rounded characters. 50% might not feature in the film, but brainstorming character and plot might lead to story points and fuel conflict. Deepen your film by just showing the iceberg tip of a character trait using a subtle reveal.

Giving the character a choice or some kind of dilemma enables them to be revealed and defined. Something has to happen to them so that we can see how they react and reveal their particular traits. In your own life, see how others treat and react to people who they don't have to be nice to: the waiter who spills the wine, the cab driver who drives too slow, the newspaper boy who delivers a soggy, ripped paper. Our own characters are revealed in adverse or stressful situations. Some panic, some are calm, some look to others. A character that is considered three-dimensional must have contradictory traits. In the film *3:10 to Yuma* (2007), set in the Old West, Christian Bale plays Dan Evans, a father struggling to pay the bills who is neither respected by his son nor loved by his wife. As a civilian he undertakes the mission refused by others, including law enforcement, to escort prisoner and gang leader Ben Wade (Russell Crowe) to the train station to catch the 3:10 to Yuma and then prison. Along the way he'll have to fight off Wade's gang as they try to rescue their leader. Both characters are multifaceted; Bale plows through his fears in a bid to earn his son's respect. It's Crowe's villain who is perhaps even more intriguing — he recognizes Bale's character's plight and *even helps Bale to get him to the station*! Crowe's character knows he can easily escape once on the train, but having the hero and the villain pursue the same thing is genius writing and character building. There's more to Crowe's villain than meets the eye, making his relationship with Bale an interesting one.

In everyday life, we exhibit a whole host of traits and characteristics. But in the movies, characters need to display only a few of the important ones to help us understand who they are. We can then assume a host of other traits that might go along with it. It's okay to write characters who are sexist, racist, or even weak, male or female, since that may be what the film or scene requires. It doesn't mean you're endorsing that behavior or setting back a movement. Don't get too hung up on writing characters reflecting what is currently in vogue, and don't be bound by societal norms. All characters, men or women, can be strong, shy, tough, manipulative, weak, egotistical, or possess any trait you wish so long as they're believable and well developed. As long as your characters make the audience *feel* something, then you've done your job. If a female character is weak and neurotic but believable and interesting, great! If she's disciplined, decisive, and kicks ass, then great! If a male character is chauvinist, arrogant, and a racist, great — *if he's believable and makes the audience feel something.* Writing a "strong" character doesn't necessarily mean they go around throwing punches, having an attitude, and kicking down doors. It's also being mentally strong, assertive, and steadfast. It could be defiantly standing up

to the boss, abusive partner, or court ruling. Their strength is shown by their refusal to concede, standing up after being physically or mentally thrown to the floor.

Sarah Connor (Linda Hamilton) in *Terminator 2: Judgment Day* (1991) is considered a three-dimensional character for a number of reasons. Connor has an unwavering focus to achieve her objective, one that has consumed her adult life. She even attempts to blow up the computer factory, which lands her to an insane asylum fighting for her cause. She possesses a strong (if sometimes warped) mind, a tough attitude, a lot of motivation, and a singular point of view. She's obsessed with Skynet creator Miles Dyson and his company Cyberdyne, fixated on killing him to prevent the nuclear-holocaust future she sees in her nightmares. She almost becomes the machine she's been fighting. However deep her commitment, when the time comes to hold a gun to Dyson's head, she's conflicted. Connor can save the future, but having to take a life to do so brings out her humanity. She may be obsessed, but she's also a mother, and has emotions and a conscience like the rest of us. A host of contradictory traits make her interesting and believable.

Perhaps the central question of any character is: What do they *want*? What drives them? This want suggests a host of traits. Some characters want

1.1. Linda Hamilton as Sarah Connor in *Terminator 2: Judgment Day* (1991). A good example of a three-dimensional character.

world domination (deceitful / angry / violent); or to save the hostages (compassionate / caring / optimistic); or to protect their family (vigilant / serious / responsible); or to kill the president (hostile / diligent / bold); or to sit around all day and play video games (lazy / apathetic). Not everyone with these desires also has these traits, but they're good starting points.

After the protagonist and the antagonist come secondary characters and friends. On the outskirts, we have the minor roles that might have one or two lines and make a fleeting appearance. Secondary characters also have to be introduced and defined, but not as much as the main protagonist does. Try to give each character a distinctive voice. Of course, if you have more of an ensemble piece, with four or five main roles, then each of them needs to be defined and brought to life. Characters with smaller roles and

less screen time can be somewhat stereotypical; the audience needs to know who they are watching, and fast. Time doesn't allow for a more in-depth analysis, and it's just efficient storytelling. The interfering mother-in-law, the blue-collar taxi driver, the stuck-up hotel manager . . . If we find out that the doctor who has four lines of dialogue talking to the protagonist is going through a divorce, what impact does this have on the story? If the answer is none whatsoever, then we don't need it. It adds nothing, confusing the audience as to why it might be important. Sometimes actors in these minor roles like to embellish their part with a made-up backstory. However, the details of this will never be conveyed, and an awkward performance is what emerges on screen.

What histories do the secondary characters have with the protagonist? What traits do they bring out in them? What is their relationship? This is where writing out character biographies before you start the script — a paragraph of their history, background, and most importantly how they relate to the protagonist — might help. Over the course of the script, try to put the main characters through every form of emotion; it's through their interactions with the secondary characters that these can be explored further. Not only do we get to see the characters in various situations, but it's how they react to these events that enable the characters to shine through. Running through the emotional gamut also makes a part exciting for an actor. Ask how your character relates to the theme of the film too. What is it that they do, know, act, or say that ties in with the overall story themes?

BACKSTORY

The writer needs to solidly understand what happened to each of the main characters before the current story began. This gives them a three-dimensional edge and makes them more human and believable. What's their history? Are they an orphan? Were they a solider in the war? Have they been divorced three times? Their past experiences might affect their present-day reactions. As a writer, you don't need to know or create everything. Most details won't be relevant, but is there something that does pertain to the present day that you can use? There are the lazy shorthand approaches — divorced, alcoholic, lost a child — to be avoided. They are still valid, but how can you tweak and differentiate them from what has come before? What else could be troubling or burdening them?

The protagonist's character should be clear from the actions they take in the present and not rely on backstory to give us that information. Every writer has his or her own tricks for deftly weaving in backstory. Can it be done visually rather than spoken, which would be the preferred method? Let's look at a few alternatives. The Mel Gibson thriller *Blood Father* (2016) takes an interesting approach by having Gibson share his backstory in the opening few lines. How do the filmmakers get away with this? It's all part of a confession at Alcoholics Anonymous. A crafty, effective way of giving us everything we need to know. Characters in Christopher Nolan's *Dunkirk* (2017) have little or no backstory whatsoever. Nolan contended that the film was not about if characters had girlfriends or wives back home, but how they reacted to the bombs dropping around them. "Biography is unimportant in such circumstances," Nolan says.

INTRODUCTION TO CHARACTER

How we are first introduced to the main character is a prime consideration. What are they doing when we first see them? These first moments are very important; characters establish identities, and the audience decides with whom they'll connect. The scene description of the protagonist's entrance is always exciting to write. The hero or heroine has just walked onstage! Write for the star, and look after the star at all times. Consider writer Randall Wallace's introduction to the character of William Wallace in Mel Gibson's *Braveheart* (1995):

```
Riding along the road comes
William Wallace. Grown now,
a man. He sits on his horse
as if born there, his back
straight, his hands relaxed
on the reins. He has a look
of lean, rippled power. He
looks dangerous.
```

We get a good idea of who this person might be, and can infer a lot too. Notice how there isn't too much exact physical description, either; instead, we get more of a feeling of who he is — calm, relaxed, secure, confident. There are some external and internal attributes here. In addition, too much detail in your character description might limit your casting options.

Always consider what the antagonist is doing the first time they appear. In Michael Bay's action extravaganza *The Rock* (1996), the first character we see (and are asked to identify with, which is uncommon) is the villain, Ed Harris's General Hummel. We find him putting flowers on his wife's grave, asking forgiveness for the actions he's about to take: holding the city of San Francisco for ransom by threatening its people with poison gas. A villain with a conscience! We could have seen the villain randomly killing someone or executing a similarly evil deed, but he instead comes off as three-dimensional, contradictory, and human — his motives are understandable and sympathetic.

Consider not just the character description, for the best way to convey character is actually through action. As a writer or director, how can we present a character *visually*? In everyday life we learn about people by looking at what they *do*, not what they *say*. Someone might talk about doing something, like visiting the gym or volunteering, but whether they actually do so is the true test.

In the 1997 action film *Air Force One*, we are introduced to Harrison Ford as U.S. President just before he is about to give a speech at the Russian embassy. Ford is a few lines into his prewritten speech when, to the horror of his support team, he puts it away and improvises the rest. He speaks from the heart about recent tragedies, and vows to put a stop to them. His actions show us he can improvise in the moment, that he doesn't necessarily do what's he's been prepared for, and that he has a genuine, vested interest in solving the issues at hand, not just telling people what they want to hear.

In *Silence of the Lambs* (1991), screenwriter Ted Tally has the head of the prison facility explain serial killer Hannibal Lecter's character and history to visiting FBI agent Clarice Starling as she is escorted through dark basement tunnels to see him. This would normally be a no-no, but we allow it as the details are so shocking and intense. It juxtaposes nicely with finally seeing Lecter in the flesh; he isn't hiding in the shadows or trying to be mysterious,

but standing in the center of his cell, patiently waiting, visually contradicting the aural description. It's the exact opposite of what we were expecting — character through *inaction*, if you like. How can what we have just heard match this calm and gentle man before us? This approach is now even scarier to both Starling and the audience.

One of my favorite character introductions on film is of Morgan Freeman's "Somerset" in the movie *Se7en* (1995). We see Somerset's morning routine — he gracefully puts on his tie and buttons up his shirt. His bedside table hosts a napkin, a police badge, a knife, a pen, and his gun, all neatly laid out. He gently removes a speck of dust from his jacket before putting it on, turning out the bedside lamp, and leaving to start his day. Not

1.2. Anthony Hopkins as Hannibal Lecter in *Silence of the Lambs* (1991).

1.3. Character through action. Somerset (Morgan Freeman) visually tells us everything we need to know about him in *Se7en* (1995).

a word spoken — but we know this man is calm, methodical, organized, prepared, and well groomed.

Consider the introduction of Mel Gibson's Benjamin Martin character in *The Patriot* (2000). Later we'll see Gibson's Martin character lead the Colonial Militia against the British during the American Revolution of 1776, but before that, he's a widower and family man, raising his children.

When we first see him, he's in the final stages of constructing a wooden chair after hours of crafting, sanding, and molding the pieces together. His children watch expectantly as Martin tries to sit in it for the first time. The chair holds for a second or two before collapsing, sending Martin crashing to the floor! In a fit of frustration he throws the broken pieces into the corner of the barn, joining the pile of

1.4. Mel Gibson in *The Patriot* (2000).

splintered wood and broken timber from previous failed attempts! It's a humorous scene that allows the audience to warm and relate to Gibson's character. Why do we relate to him? Because he's fallible. He messes things up, just like we do. He's not perfect; if he must fail at something, let it be making chairs, not leading an army — which we will need him to excel at later in the film. This introduction also shows us that he's not a quitter. The pile of broken chair parts not only provides a punchline to the joke, but also shows how many (unsuccessful) attempts Gibson has made at building this chair. He has tenacity.

Director Richard Donner goes in the opposite direction with his action thriller *16 Blocks* (2006). Down-and-out cop Jack Mosley (Bruce Willis) is not respected within his police unit because of his lethargic manner and drinking problem. Mosley's introduction in the film swiftly follows one of his fellow officers securing a crime scene in an apartment complex and asking, "Who's downstairs we don't need?" We then cut to:

1.5. The empty frame as the audience awaits Jack Mosley (Bruce Willis) in *16 Blocks* (2006).

We hold on this empty handheld shot for three or four seconds before Willis makes an appearance, limping his way up the stairs to the crime scene. The framing and editing tell us a lot here. The editor could have cut into the shot just as Willis appears, but we come in earlier than that. The audience (and other characters) must wait for Willis because he's so slow.

1.6. Willis finally arrives on screen in *16 Blocks* (2006).

The top step's the obstructive foreground element, blocking the lower half of the shot too. It's like the camera doesn't even respect our hero, and the operator can't be bothered to frame him correctly! Of course, later in the movie when Willis's character needs to step up to protect his charge about to testify, he delivers and becomes the man and officer he should be.

What is the first thing we see your main character doing? Can it be something visual that shows us who they are? What character traits are evident through the actions that they take? People and characters are judged on what they *do*, not what they *say*. In most cases you're introducing your character in a heroic manner to signify that the star just walked on screen.

CHARACTER ARC AND CHANGE

Every main character should ideally change over the course of the story. In order to see this change or "arc," the original state of the character must be established early in the story. Maybe it's their outlook, their beliefs, or their prejudices. Maybe it's whether they are capable of doing something physical, like fighting or boxing or building something, and we chart their progress throughout the film. So these changes can be internal or physical, but they must happen and are best shown through some kind of filmable action or behavior. Characters and their relationships must develop over time. People grow fond of each other, or grow apart, but the audience must see these things happen. They can't just occur in the minds of the characters, or the production's actors or director. Your characters must be left in a different place than how we first found them.

MOTIVATIONS

The script of the blockbuster hit *Batman* (1989) called for Jack Nicholson's Joker to drag Vicki Vale (Kim Basinger) to the top of the cathedral in Gotham City in the finale of the film. On set, Nicholson asked director Tim Burton, "Why am I walking up these stairs? Where am I going?" and Burton replied, "We'll talk about it when you get to the top." Burton added, "I had to tell him I didn't know . . ."

What's driving your characters to do what they do? What do they "want"? Every line, action, and movement from a character, no matter how small, must be motivated in some way. All of their actions are getting them closer to what they desire. If your character does something "uncharacteristic" solely to get out of a tricky storyline or into a spectacular action sequence, your script needs to find an alternative. I've written myself into corners where the bad guys need to find out where the hero is hiding. A character makes some silly mistake or does something uncharacteristic or highly coincidental to facilitate this maneuver. Sloppy writing! Some scripts even start production as a series of action scenes and available locations; the writer must connect the dots and create a coherent story. Knowing what has to happen in this way can lead to poor coincidences, or characters doing silly things just to justify the action you have planned. Make sure everything is character-centric first, with character choices fueling any action.

THE HERO MUST BE IN THE KNOW

Your lead characters must be in the know to some degree. We like our heroes knowledgeable, confident, and wise. If they don't know what to do, they are no better than us, and we feel vulnerable. The audience wants the character to lead, even if they are not consciously aware of this desire. We want someone we can all figuratively hide behind who confidently knows the way out when all hell breaks loose. They shouldn't be ignorant of what might lie ahead either; you need to protect the star of your film. The makers of the James Bond franchise do this very well, as when Bond is called into M's office and asked what he knows about a particular supervillain. Bond then confidently gives us the villain's background off the top of his head. We now know the information, and our hero was the smart one who provided it. We don't really want our hero asking lots of questions.

A good example of a lead character being smart and ahead of the game occurs in *Angels & Demons*

(2009), starring Tom Hanks as Robert Langdon. We open with Langdon swimming in the Harvard University pool. In between strokes, he comes up for air and spots a strange figure walking alongside the pool. Langdon spies a relevant insignia on the person's briefcase. He stops and addresses the man, but doesn't ask, "Who are you?" Instead Langdon comments, "A swim might help your jetlag . . . the bags under your eyes. It's five in the morning and you're from the Vatican." Langdon is smart and ahead of the game, and no questions have been asked.

There are helpful techniques even if our heroes don't know all of what needs to be known. Take *Indiana Jones and the Last Crusade* (1989). The audience needs to know what lies ahead, and what artifact Indy is chasing. We have a scene where Indy (Harrison Ford) meets Walter Donovan (Julian Glover), a collector

1.7. Tom Hanks (Robert Langdon) is ahead of the game in *Angels & Demons* (2009).

of antiquities who asks Indy to help him find the Holy Grail. (He also turns out to be the villain of the piece.) The scene is chock full of exposition, all that important information we the audience need to understand. Yet we can't just sit back and listen as Donovan tells our hero and the audience what they need to know. That would be boring, and we need Indy to do better. Donovan reveals only *half* the info before Indy butts in: "I've heard this bedtime story before . . ." and then tells Donovan (and us) the rest of what we need to know. The scene is therefore nicely split, with each character revealing information to us — but also with Indy, most importantly, being in the know.

If our hero is not in the know because the information is highly technical or scientific, be careful about how they find it out. The worst thing you can do is have your hero ask lots of questions and get talked at by the person who does know. We are figuratively sitting next to them in the same class, on the same level as our "all-knowing" hero. Let's revisit Tom Hanks in *Angels & Demons* as he dodges this bullet very well. A dangerous canister of antimatter has been stolen from a lab and may be used in a bomb to blow up half of Rome. Hanks's Robert Langdon character has been summoned to track it down. He finds himself at the Vatican waiting to meet Commander Richter

of the Swiss Guard (Stellan Skarsgard) to discuss a way forward. Scientist and antimatter expert Dr. Vittoria Vetra (Ayelet Zurer) has also just arrived to warn the Commander about the stolen canister's volatility. Writers David Koepp and Akiva Goldsman and director Ron Howard cleverly have Hanks stand behind Dr. Vetra while she explains everything about the canister to the Commander, who can then reasonably ask all the important questions. Hanks (and us) then learn all we need to know without Hanks's Langdon character looking ignorant. It's all about saving face and making your character and star look good — but don't take this unquestioning-hero thing too literally. Obviously, at some point the hero does and will ask a question or two, especially if the character is a police detective or similar occupation. When they do, make sure it's not about the really important stuff and not at a time when you can pass that question to someone else.

TAKING ACTION

At some time in your story, your character must decide to take positive action. They can only tolerate their situation so long before they must take a decisive step forward. The bully pushes and pushes before the protagonist decides to do something about it; the wife in an abusive relationship has had enough of her marriage and decides to leave; the unjustly accused man on the run must stop running and proactively go after the people who set him up. This shows strength of character, and turns the protagonist into someone the audience can get behind and support. Find a way of showing this change in the character's mindset and visually depicting their decisive moment. Do they stand and walk out to show their decision? Do they push that button? Speed off in the car? Or sit back in a chair, fold their arms, and do nothing? These expressions of inaction prove that the character has decided to change. Any big decision must be made by the hero of the piece. A secondary character can't say, "Let's go kill the monster! Follow me!" and have the hero reply, "That's a good idea. Let's do that." The hero or lead must make any decision or have the big speech, and show visually and physically what needs to be done. Protect the star at all costs.

SETUPS AND PAYOFFS

Setups and payoffs are great devices for screenwriters to extricate their characters from difficult situations or even save the day. The setup or "plant" is an object, skill, device, weapon, or tool that is planted or presented to the audience early on, and then called back into action when it's most needed. The trick is not to plant it too late in the game and have the payoff fairly soon after as it might seem contrived. Plant it too early, and the audience may forget about it. Let's look at some examples:

In the Tom Cruise movie *Jack Reacher* (2012), Cruise is an ex-military investigator looking for a killer who shot five random victims in the street. Cruise works alongside lawyer Helen (Rosamund Pike), and in one scene we see that Pike's character stores all her related case files in boxes in the back of her car. Later on, when Cruise uses her car to escape the villains shooting at him, he finds the boxes of paper handy in protecting him from the haze of bullets. Set up and paid off.

In the action film *RoboCop* (1987), we see newbie cop Murphy (Peter Weller) shot to pieces by the bad guys in a warehouse raid. He's then turned into RoboCop — part man, part machine. Back on the streets with his memory wiped, he cleans the city of all its bad elements. He malfunctions a little and begins to recall the faces of the bad guys who shot him. Halfway through the story, RoboCop strides into police headquarters to download some recordings he's made of one of the villains he's just encountered. A sharp attachment jolts out of his knuckles, and he uses it to plug into the computer database. Later, when RoboCop tracks down the bad guys and takes his revenge, he finds himself

1.8. *RoboCop* (1987) sets up this sharp attachment hidden in his knuckles as a way to kill the villain in the finale.

up against the lead villain, Clarence Boddicker, who has RoboCop pinned down without his gun. How does RoboCop get out of this predicament? He shoots the dagger-like computer connector from his knuckles straight into Boddicker's neck. RoboCop gets his revenge; now it's all up close and personal, not simply firing his gun from 150 feet away. Planted and paid off nicely. The trick to setups and payoffs is to determine what tool or object will save the day at film's end, then reverse-engineer your storyline to strategically plant that item where it will do the most good.

REVERSALS

Let's talk about "reversals." Reversals are a wonderful tool in the scriptwriter's arsenal, and I absolutely love watching them on screen. Reversals invert expectations for the audience. A surprise with a twist: the audience gets a little bit ahead of the film, which then goes in the opposite direction. Earlier setups have satisfying, unexpected payoffs, all driven by the reversal. They can add tension, help character, and move the story along. One of my favorite reversals comes from the comedy *City Slickers* (1991). It's nicely set up early in the film. Depressed and nearly forty, Billy Crystal and friends go on a life-changing cattle drive across the open plains of the West to get some perspective on life. They ride, eat underneath the stars, and are cowboys for two weeks, moving cattle from one ranch to another. Early on we see that Crystal's character can't rope or lasso the cattle. Everyone else can but him. It's embarrassing. He tries throughout the film, but to no avail. In an action-packed finale, while moving cattle across a dangerous river on horseback, one of the baby calves gets caught in the current and swept down the river! Crystal yee-ha's outta there and gallops down the side of the riverbank, preparing his rope to lasso and save the screaming calf . . . There's tension because the audience knows he can't lasso. He swings the rope above his head, galloping hard, waiting for that perfect time. Finally, at just the right moment, he releases, catching the calf! Success! Now, here's where the reversal comes in. A character's change must be believable. If we've set up that Crystal's character can't lasso, and he still can't during his crucial moment, he's learned nothing and disappoints the audience. And if we set him up as unable to lasso but then he suddenly can, saving the day, it's cheesy and predictable. So what do the filmmakers do? A reversal. He lassos, captures the calf, then gets pulled into the water himself! From a character point of view, he's changed for the better, but the film suggests he's not out of trouble and actually in more danger, since Crystal and the calf are then caught up in the tide. The third option now sees Crystal's character rescued by his friends, who are on this journey with him. They all string together from the riverbank and reach out, grabbing his arm. Whoa! What a sequence, and what fantastic writing.

EXPOSITION

Here's a tough one. This is where your skill as a writer really comes into its own. The audience must know the exposition — that awkward bit of information that hooks a viewer into a scene. Imagine having a scene where a man and a woman are walking down the street talking. Are they husband and wife, brother and sister, just good friends? The man might say, "Mom called. She said you haven't visited in a while." Can we now assume they are brother and sister? Probably, but it could be his mother they are discussing, and the woman is an old neighbor who once lived next to the mother. Strangers in a scene can ask questions all the time, and this can be a good way of sneaking in the information we need to know. Friends and relatives can't, and seldom do, ask those questions.

Infusing a scene with information is also accomplished through onscreen text, narration, or the reading aloud of a letter or similar communique. Bad exposition occurs when a character talks to themselves. A solitary character looks through old photos and solves the mystery, declaring, "Oh my! So Michael *was* killed by his neighbor when he found out about the affair! I gotta warn Rachel!" If anything too technical or scientific occurs, a knowing third party or surrogate audience member can ask questions for the audience. One scientist probably wouldn't ask these questions of the other; they both already know the answers. This third party could be a news reporter, a child, or maybe we see the technical character giving a presentation to an audience. The tornado movie *Twister* (1996) uses the third-party device very well. Helen Hunt and Bill Paxton play two scientists chasing tornadoes to study their characteristics and effects. They discuss lots of scientific and technical information that would just go over the audience's head. So what do writers Michael Crichton and Anne-Marie Martin do? Put Bill Paxton's new girlfriend in the car, asking Hunt and Paxton questions about all the technical meteorology mumbo-jumbo while pursuing Paxton to get Hunt's signature on divorce papers. Exposition is tough and needs to be snuck past the audience. *The skill comes in burying the exposition in the dialogue so we don't know we've absorbed it.* If the delivery is too clunky or on the nose, the audience will suspect the content is important, possibly using it to guess the ending of the film.

A good way to squeeze exposition past the audience is to have one character use it as ammunition against another in an argument. The audience won't notice important information since they'll be too focused on character reactions. Show, don't tell, the exposition. Tell your story visually.

Exposition doesn't just happen at the beginning either. Good writing has exposition still being drip-fed right up to the finale. It keeps the story interesting since we're still finding information out and not just watching some characters kiss or buildings being blown up.

BUDGET

If you're writing a script to practice your craft, write what you want: spaceships, boat chases, epic battles. In the more likely event that you are writing something you'll also be producing, know what can be achieved within your budgetary parameters. Things costs money, even the little things you don't think cost money, cost money. In fact it's those things you need to be most wary of. Even writing:

EXT. FIELD — NIGHT

. . . might cause you or your producer a few headaches. The producer will then be considering power, lighting, cold weather, health, and safety, and that's all before the scene dictates: "The cars blow to pieces beneath the alien ship." My ambition has gotten me unstuck a few times, so I'm not about to say what you can and can't write, but you don't want to force your movie-going audience to immediately make concessions. Even the smallest of variables in the script can create expenses, behind-the-scenes work, and headaches. In my last book, I told the story of a student script that started with:

```
EXT. STREET — NIGHT

The four police cars
come to a screeching halt
outside the burning house.
```

All this would involve: blocking off the street, filming at night, power, lighting, working with local residents, sourcing police cars and uniforms, finding a house to set up our special-effect fire . . .

So keep one eye on the page and one eye on the budget, especially if you're making this blockbuster your-self. Which leads us nicely to . . .

WRITING ACTION

Writing a big set piece or action sequence can be fun, but these scenes can become very boring. Audiences deserve more than just people shooting, driving fast, or throwing things at each other. The action needs to escalate and evolve, and the stakes need to be raised, or an action scene can die fast. Like the film as a whole, a smaller action sequence needs to have a beginning, middle, and end.

First up is "style." How you write the action on the page dictates how it will translate to screen. *Short, sharp descriptions give readers a sense of pace and help them read the text faster.* Don't make the reader wade through lines and lines of dense details; they might lose the sense of jeopardy, or worse, get bored.

Here's a good tip: *Think of each line of description as being one shot in the film.* By writing this way, you're subliminally inviting the reader to see each line as a separate unit of action with a cut in between. Let's take a look:

```
EXT. FREEWAY — NIGHT

MICHAEL pulls down hard on
the steering wheel.

Tires screech as the
Lamborghini effortlessly
spins one hundred and
eighty degrees.

Fist tight around the
stick, as Michael throws it
into REVERSE.

His foot SLAMS on the gas
pedal.
```

```
Speeding backwards now,
Michael turns his steely-
eyed focus out the
shattered rear window.

The black SUV races up
behind him, getting closer.
```

Each one of these lines is a new shot. It's written in cuts, which helps the director see what you want them to see. There's even the odd word in capitals to help emphasize things.

Next let's look at "priorities." Within an action sequence, the protagonist's "want" should be constantly changing. There might be an overall aim, but underneath that are smaller things that take priority. These changing priorities keep the action scene alive. Take the finale of *Indiana Jones and the Last Crusade* (1989). The overall aim is for Indy (Harrison Ford) to rescue his dad (Sean Connery) from "the belly of that steel beast," a German tank, but many obstacles pop up that change his priorities along the way:

First, while on horseback, riding alongside the moving tank, Indy has to avoid the tank's shells being fired at him.

Next, escape the German soldiers chasing him.

Then take out the tank's gun by disabling it.

Then avoid getting shot by the SS officer on top of the tank.

Once he's jumped on the tank, he has to fight more soldiers.

Then fight hand to hand with the SS officer.

Then hang on to the disabled tank gun and not get crushed by an approaching rock.

Then get his dad out of the tank turret.

Then fight with the SS officer again.

Then stop his dad from falling under the tank's tracks, achieved by slinging his whip around his dad's leg, all while still fighting the SS officer.

1.9. Harrison Ford as Indiana Jones having his priorities changed in *Indiana Jones and the Last Crusade* (1989).

Finally, he must get off the tank before it drives over the cliff edge.

The stakes keep rising, and something new is always being added to the equation to keep things moving. If the protagonist's want stays the same, the scene becomes stale. Each action has a consequence, and the subsequent reaction consistently moves the story forward. Ask: *What has now changed because of that fight, chase, or destruction?* These layered action scenes can be very tough to plan and structure, as can making sure each action causes an equal reaction that changes the direction of the scene.

THE VILLAIN OF THE PIECE

In most cases, a film is only as good as the villain. If the villain is weak, the film is weak. If the villain is formidable, then the film is stronger for it. How could you write your antagonist to make your film stronger? Villains don't think they're villains. They're not playing evil; they're just doing what needs to be done to forward their agenda.

First, get the villain in early so they can announce their plan and the film can really start. Our hero, whoever they may be, can't react or stop something if that *something* hasn't been declared. The hero needs something substantial to rebel against. We might not even see the villain (as in the forthcoming *Skyfall* example), but we *must see the results of their actions.* They're blowing things up, or manipulating the action from behind the scene. Obviously, good villains don't have to be human either. Look at the liquid-metal T-1000 from *Terminator 2: Judgment Day* (1991) or the aliens from the *Alien* franchise. To quote the cyborg Ash from *Alien* (1979): "I admire its purity. A survivor . . . unclouded by conscience, remorse, or delusions of morality." Nice character description of a good villain right there. Other notable villains include Hans Gruber (Alan Rickman) in *Die Hard* (1988) and Clarence Boddicker (Kurtwood Smith) in *RoboCop* (1987).

Here's an example of a truly formidable villain that presents a very clear and present danger — Philip Seymour Hoffman as Owen Davian in *Mission: Impossible III* (2006). He's strong, intelligent, and ruthless. He's on screen from the opening scene and immediately threatens Tom Cruise's Ethan Hunt character. Hoffman's Davian is simply terrifying; there's no reasoning with him and he's prepared to sacrifice everything and everyone to get what he wants.

Contrast this with the next film in the franchise, *Mission: Impossible — Ghost Protocol* (2011), where the villain doesn't appear on screen for 29 minutes. When we do see him it's only via a TV set, speaking Russian.

We're not given much chance to connect or get a solid understanding of his devious motives. The next time we see him he's pretending to be someone else by wearing a mask. From the audience's point of view, he's still off screen. His objective is a little generic — he wants to set off nuclear missiles — and to top it all off, Cruise's Ethan Hunt character doesn't even kill him in the finale; he kills himself! Not much satisfaction for the audience. I'm a fan of the *Mission: Impossible* movies and Cruise, but this poorly developed villain made the film one of the weaker installments. Thankfully the pendulum swings back the other way in *Mission: Impossible — Rogue Nation* (2015); the villain kills an innocent record store clerk in front of a helpless Cruise nine minutes into the film.

"Silva," the villain in the James Bond film *Skyfall* (2012), is played by Javier Bardem. Although we don't see Silva on screen for over an hour, which should be damaging, the effects of his plan are immediately clear. He has a presence and this is the difference. An ex-agent, Silva's backstory is strong and intertwined with Bond and MI6. Compare this with the next Bond film, *Spectre* (2015). The villain of the piece is Blofeld (Christoph Waltz), and he sits in the shadows literally and figuratively, not really doing much. Bond goes looking for him, but Blofeld presents no real immediate threat, unlike Silva. Bond could theoretically take two weeks off from looking for Blofeld, go skiing or on vacation, and then resume his hunt; it wouldn't matter since there is no sense of urgency to hold our interest. These are minor considerations that can add up to the audience feeling somewhat underwhelmed. It's worth noting that *Skyfall* was commercially and critically more widely accepted than *Spectre*.

1.10. Christoph Waltz sits in the shadows in *Spectre* (2015).

Things are stronger still if the hero and villain know each other. Consider the Sam Raimi *Spider-Man* films. The hero *knows* the villain, as they're friends! Their backstories are related, and this makes the story have more emotional wallop and the action so much more layered. Spider-Man is not just fighting the villain, but someone he knows and cares about. Other examples where the hero knows the villain include *Star Wars* (1977), *Raiders of the Lost Ark* (1981), *GoldenEye* (1995), and *X-Men* (2000). All commercially successful and critically well-received movies. The lightsaber battles between Luke Skywalker and Darth Vader in the finales of *The Empire Strikes Back* (1980) and *Return of the Jedi* (1983) are so much more than just swordfights between hero and villain since we know they're really father versus son.

HAVE A HEART

At the center of any good story is emotion. Weaving an emotional core throughout your script will give your story some much-needed heart. Heart can fuel your story and give your characters more depth, meaning, and drive to support their actions. Your characters need to make us *feel* something, be it joy, fear, or sorrow. They must make us cry — or cry with laughter. Films are essentially about relationships, either intimate, platonic, or familial, and with relationships come a host of feelings. Have you ever watched a film and thought something was missing? The action was there, the story was there, but somehow you didn't care, and it all felt a little . . . flat? You just watched; you weren't involved. Chances are there was no heart. Tom Hanks formed a "relationship" with

1.11. Luke Skywalker and his father, Darth Vader, battle it out in *The Empire Strikes Back* (1980).

a volleyball named Wilson while stranded on an island in *Cast Away* (2000) and made moviegoers cry when he lost him at sea. So how do we weave this heart into our scripts? *Start with what the character's want.* Their want is what drives them. Ask how their want or objective is tied to what has happened, or what could happen. Anything that threatens to prevent that or even take it away is the key to their heart. But go too far the other way and you're at risk of manipulating the audience's feelings, and then things just turn mushy. Heart is good; sentimentality is not.

Family is primal; everyone can relate to it and grasp the theme immediately. It finds its way into a lot of good stories. Russell Crowe's Maximus is fighting to avenge his family in *Gladiator* (2000); hitman *John Wick* (2014) is drawn out of retirement to take revenge on the thugs that killed the dog his recently departed wife bought for him; Jodie Foster is protecting her daughter in *Panic Room* (2002); *RoboCop* (1987) begins to remember his old family and visits his previous home only to find it now abandoned; Harrison Ford's U.S. President fights to protect his family on board *Air Force One* (1997); Matthew McConaughey has to decide whether to leave his family and go into space to save humanity in *Interstellar* (2014); in *Terminator 2: Judgment Day* (1991)

Linda Hamilton is protecting her son from the Terminator; Bruce Willis's John McClane is fighting the terrorists in *Die Hard* (1988), but his wife is among the hostages. Even Vin Diesel fights and drives fast cars to protect and support his extended family in the *Fast and the Furious* franchise.

Giving the protagonist a personal stake in the proceedings gives the film heart. What personal stake would give your story more of an emotional wallop?

CREATING WORLDS

We might associate blockbusters with glossy, stylized visuals and a hit song, but what they all do very well is create a world. What do we mean by that? Films like *Star Wars* (1977), or what novelist J.K. Rowling created with the Harry Potter books, later to be adapted into films (2001–2011), create whole new worlds with their own myths, orders, traditions, and rules. The writer must know everything about this new world, but doesn't necessarily need to show it all and certainly doesn't need to put it all in the script. Show us just enough of the tip of the iceberg to speculate what lies beneath it. There's no need to take the audience all the way through it; they lack the attention span and you don't have the running time. A whole world has been created, and you're just interested in telling a story set within that world, so some of the rules and traditions might not matter. Not all of your work and research must be seen or heard. This glimpse of the new world could be: a billion-dollar Wall Street company, a magical faraway land, a mob family, a spy agency, a dangerous ghetto, or a period of time centuries ago. They all are new worlds the general public might not have the chance to see every day.

In *John Wick* (2014) and *John Wick: Chapter 2* (2017), we see the secretive underground world of the assassin. We see that special gold coins are the currency that tailors, gunsmiths, and underground operatives in that world know and use. New assassination contracts are received using old typewriters and out-of-date computers. All superb little touches that make this world believable and visually interesting. With that world comes traditions, oaths, rules, and consequences. It's exclusive to that world, and it's exciting for the audience to be shown backstage.

Setting up these new worlds can take up a lot of screen time and exposition, so a writer must cleverly drip-feed information to the audience. A new world's logistics are best demonstrated visually; forgo characters explaining things to each other that they and the audience probably already know already. Be

mindful if your story is set in the world of science fiction or fantasy; it's easy to get carried away with traditions, the methods of secret orders, or the history of institutions or magic, all of which need to be explained for the story to make sense.

Sometimes scripts benefit from starting with some sort of action. Setting up new worlds and providing exposition can take time. Opening with action keeps audiences interested, and the action's motives and purpose can be explained later. Inaugural action scenes also explain the rules of your new world using visual shorthand.

AUDIENCES' EXPECTATIONS — GIVE THEM WHAT THEY WANT

Russian playwright Anton Chekhov said once in a letter to a friend, "If in the first act you have hung a pistol on the wall, then in the following act it should be fired. Otherwise don't put it there." Audiences' expectations are important to adhere to. Even if the outcome you are promising might seem clichéd, you still need to deliver. It's how you deliver on your promise that can make things interesting. The action movie *Speed* (1994) centers on a bomb on a bus that will go off if the vehicle drops beneath 50 miles per hour. The bomb *must* be detonated by the end of the

1.12. *Speed* (1994) giving the audience what it wants.

film. It can't just be defused, and the bus pull into a rest stop, once that setup has been established. How much of an anticlimax would that be? So not only does the bus get blown up, it crashes into an enormous freight plane on the airport runway! The bomb on the bus is Chekhov's pistol hung on the wall.

Sometimes films deliver the bang even when their hero's job is to prevent the bang from happening. Confusing? Well, we do need to see something kind of spectacle, but we can't if our hero is smart and stops it. So how can we have both? We blow up the bomb within a bomb. The George Clooney actioner *The Peacemaker* (1997) and the James Bond film *A View to a Kill* (1985) see the hero manage to blow up the explosive device of the bomb itself, but not the nuclear element attached to it that will cause the massive destruction the villain intended. The

audience gets their explosion and the hero the credit for stopping a larger blast. In the action thriller *Jack Ryan: Shadow Recruit* (2014), the titular hero (Chris Pine) drives a truck carrying a live bomb into a river. We prevent the bomb causing massive damage to Wall Street, but still get our bang in the water. *Angels & Demons* (2009) sees the antimatter bomb device go off, but miles above Rome in a helicopter, so we prevent the planned destruction while still getting the visual spectacle.

Audiences have certain expectations in place, whether they are aware of them or not. Audiences expect to see the cop chase the serial killer around a dark tunnel by the finale; they expect to see the bomb go off in one way or another — however clichéd you think that might be. Don't be too clever and deny them what they bought the admission ticket for.

THE STARS AND THEIR SIXTH SENSE

What do we mean by a star's sixth sense? The hero needs to be ahead of the curve. They spot the signs and always seem to have an inkling that something just ain't right . . . Let's look at an example. *The Wolverine* (2013) sees Hugh Jackman's Logan character attend the funeral of a Japanese solider he saved in the Second World War. Local thugs are in the neighborhood and are looking to kidnap the soldier's wealthy daughter. During the funeral, Jackman spots gang tattoos under the robe of one of the monks attending the service. Maybe he isn't who he appears to be. Jackman then utters the classic line "Something's not right here . . ." all before everything kicks off and the thugs attack. An action sequence ensues, one the story needs. Having Jackman know something isn't right and not be surprised like everyone else makes him smart.

We're sitting in our seats waiting and hoping for the hero to catch up with us. The star can't react at the same time as the rest of the cast either; they must surpass everyone else in the story (and the audience) in intelligence, strategy, and anticipatory thinking. They have to figure it out, if only a moment beforehand; they have to be ahead of the game.

JONATHAN DEMME'S REFRIGERATOR QUESTIONS

We've all seen those epic blockbusters that might stretch credibility, our patience, or severely bend the rules of physics. Sometimes the writer need things to happen for any number of reasons and the road to get there might not be completely logical. *Silence of the Lambs* (1991) and *Philadelphia* (1993) director Jonathan Demme had a wonderful label for any issues of logic or cheating you might be worried about in the story. Maybe it's the detailed way a character escapes from prison or discovers a crucial piece of information, anything that might raise a question in the audience's mind. It could be that the information seems to hold water and make sense, but under scrutiny smells questionable and solving it is causing you a few headaches. Demme calls these "refrigerator questions." Basically, if you go to the cinema, watch the movie, drive home, open the refrigerator, and only then say to yourself, "How did she know they were going to be home then?" or "How did he know how to do that?" then it's not important. However, if you think the audience might be asking those questions when they are still in the cinema, then that needs to be addressed in the script or on set and sorted out.

CHAPTER 2

PRODUCING YOUR BLOCKBUSTER

"You have to be a self-starter, initiating every phone call, soliciting every meeting — as many as it takes to get the answer you want or the results you need."
— LAWRENCE TURMAN, PRODUCER

My first note on being a producer is to make the movie that you want to watch. You're going to be on this project for a long time, so it has to be something you believe in, like, and would go and see if it played the local multiplex.

As a producer, you're juggling multiple areas simultaneously in your head: Costs, look / feel, locations, cast, crew, delivery dates, story, and more. The buck stops with you, so you must coordinate every detail. You're sourcing the crew and department heads from costume to make-up, from special effects to set design, from catering to camera. Producers are managing the finance and logistics, and helping to steer the project in the right creative direction, too.

During filming, the producer will be fielding problems as they arise: the catering truck hasn't turned up; that location you've booked for tomorrow just fell through; you've run out of cards / film stock; the actor isn't happy and isn't coming to set until something is settled . . . Always fighting fires.

It doesn't end there. Once filming is over, you have the post-production phase to manage. The actor has moved on to another project, and scheduling their ADR (automated dialogue replacement) is becoming a nightmare; the director is adding more visual-effect shots to the film, elevating cost; the deliverables required for foreign sales must again be rejiggered. . . . With a list like that, who would ever undertake such a job? Challenges can be fun, though, forcing you to think on your feet and solve problems. Good producers manage their schedule to get the job done.

Personal development plays a large part in producing too. You have to get not only the production in good working order, but also your own attitude. You may find yourself dealing with large organizations, named actors, agents, and financiers. You might have to go to meetings and pitch your idea or discuss what you're after. How you talk and present yourself, your vocabulary, your manners, and your etiquette all play a part. As a producer you are the public face of a production; you make the calls and take the meetings. How you come across to others is paramount. What sorts of skills are needed to perform the role of producer? Confidence, good telephone manners, tenacity, people skills, self-awareness, proactivity, persistence, calmness under pressure, diplomacy, organizational skills, and perhaps the biggest ones: preparation and anticipation. You need to be ready for the curveball that's coming at you.

This chapter features a few tips and tricks to help achieve epic blockbuster production value, and details to consider regarding script, budget, planning, locations and studios, and marketing. Now, you might be running a tight ship and doing everything by the book and officially, or you might be operating a more guerrilla filmmaking outfit and operating a little under the radar. I've done both, so I'm not going to judge. The official stance is do things correctly as a producer, but you're welcome to operate otherwise.

SCHEDULING AND BUDGET

Some say writers should write without thinking about budget so nothing hinders their creative side. But if you're making, writing, or producing a blockbuster, you can't be ignorant of scale and budget. Working at the lower end of the budgeting spectrum means you must be mindful of how much everything costs. Some expensive embellishments can be cut out, but if the pricey element is integral to the story it might not come out easily. Cutting one of the shootouts from your action movie is doable; cutting the aliens from your alien-invasion movie might be trickier.

So where do we start? Well before you move into pre-production, prepare your budget and schedule. Begin by breaking the script down page by page. Characters, locations, sets, props, special effects, visual effects, large crowd scenes, night shoots. These are the building blocks of your budget and schedule. Work out the approximate time each scene will take to film; add up those days and incorporate them into your budget. The availability of your locations and actors is another factor. When it comes to scheduling, first consider the season you're shooting. If your script is mostly daylight exteriors, filming in England between December and February won't offer much well-lit shooting time. Every scene featuring the same actors and shot at a single location should be scheduled consecutively; return trips are expensive. This level of scheduling efficiency may not always possible and may require some juggling, but it is highly cost-effective.

To begin budgeting, contact rental companies for quotes on camera and grip equipment, set construction, location fees, catering, post-production, deliverables . . . I normally inflate any areas I'm unsure of to eliminate future surprises. Work through the script with your director and department heads, and discuss how you will execute each of the scenes, then research the cost and personnel you'll need to realize them. Once you have these, punch them into your budgeting software or spreadsheet. In the post-production section, you'll need to budget for the edit and sound mix as well as any deliverables required. "Deliverables" are the separate picture and audio files and any paperwork required by distributors

should you sell your film. The sound stems containing dialogue, music, and effects tracks for foreign territories are needed so that dialogue may be dubbed. These are very important if you want your film to reach foreign audiences. Don't forget insurance on equipment rentals, your public liability for locations, and your cast and crew too. At the end of the budget, add a 10% contingency for any and all hiccups, reshoots, delays, and holdups. They *will* happen. You'll probably be a little shocked by that final figure — so let's reduce it.

BREAKING THE BANK — WHY YOUR BLOCKBUSTER DOESN'T HAVE TO BE EXPENSIVE

With the current crop of blockbusters costing between $150 and 250 million, you might assume the elements you need to make your movie will break the bank. Yes, things can add up very quickly, and budgets can skyrocket. Every movie differs, but the climate has changed dramatically over the last ten years, rendering inexpensive, useful equipment and software readily available. You can own and use the same software as all the major studios.

Now, a few hints and tips on reducing costs and teaching yourself to think and act as resourcefully as possible. Let's take a look . . .

Go through the script and limit your locations, stunts, special effects, night shoots, and crowd scenes. Don't eliminate all of them; you don't want to cut all the cool sections of your movie. But can things be reduced? Maybe instead of having two big action scenes, you have one epic one and maximize resources? It's not just the big special-effects numbers that cost big bucks; small dialogue scenes set in the middle of nowhere at night also drain funds. Those small things add up. Are there any costly one-location setups? If your character sits and looks out the window pondering their future on a moving passenger train, could they do the same thing through their home bedroom window, on the set where a host of other scenes are being shot? A character's emotional mindset is sometimes more important than where they are.

Travel costs can quickly wreck a budget. Limiting your transit time ensures more of your budget ends up on screen. Traveling itself not only costs money (gas / car and van rental / parking / tolls) but location shoots mean continually setting up and packing away all your equipment before moving on. All this is time you're not shooting. This is why some first-time filmmakers opt for one-location films. Quentin Tarantino adapted this approach when filming his breakthrough movie *Reservoir Dogs* (1992). The singular warehouse location enabled shooting to begin as soon as cast and crew were on set each morning.

Also beware of the writer throwing in the odd line of scene description that could mean hours of setup and execution time. The script might read:

```
Jane walks the corridors of
the mansion house, briefly
looking into various rooms.
```

2.1. The one-location breakthrough movie *Reservoir Dogs* (1992).

This description might necessitate four setups at locations spread across a large area. The time taken to get these four shots will greatly surpass the demands of four shots in the same room. Each shot requires lighting, grip equipment, and the movement of your crew to each new location. Discuss things with the director and break each sequence into its exact shots, considering the film's overall running time. A page of a script equates to roughly one minute of screen time. The line above reads for two lines (or one-eighth of a page), but could easily equate to 1.5 minutes of screen time. I made this mistake on a short film drama contracted for an 11-minute TV slot. Guess what happened to those expensive, sexy dolly shots of our character walking the halls of our wonderful location? They were cut.

Be economical with your locations. Can your set or location be used more than once for different scenes? Point the camera the other way, change the lighting and angles, and boom! A new set. If you're smart and consider your options, the audience will never know. I once shot in a church grave-yard. Another scene later in the movie featured an actress sitting in the back of a moving car. The talent was flying to Australia the following day, and we were about to lose her for a whole year. So we grabbed a green screen, placed it behind the car, and invited her to the church location. We shot her coverage in the church parking lot. We planned on shooting the car interiors similarly because our lead actor, the driver in the scene, could not actually drive! We worked it all out through creative thinking. Wrapping the church location and traveling overseas or using a studio to get that shot would not have worked — and would have cost time, money, and our actress.

Besides sets, what props can be reused? Director Ridley Scott (*Black Hawk Down, Alien*) tells an interesting story about his movie *The Duellists* (1977). One scene featured two actors talking as they walked alongside a mansion house. We cut before they then turn into the mansion's courtyard nearby. The art department had placed four urns along the path they were walking, and for the next shot of the characters walking into the courtyard, Scott asked for the urns to be added for decoration. The budget only allowed for the purchase of four urns, although more were needed. The crew politely reminded Scott that we had already seen the urns in the previous shot and that they couldn't appear again. Scott reminded them that it actually makes no difference, and asked how the audience *knows* they're the same urns. And what would the shot look like if production had bought eight urns and used them over the two shots? Scott realized that crew members sometimes have a psychological block and think their audience will somehow know these tricks. What can *you* reuse in your scenes? Computers, technical gear, weapons, cars, decoration, even actors?

When I was younger, I started by learning any and all software that I thought might be useful. There was editing software, and graphics packages such as Adobe After Effects and Photoshop. Big software companies often offer student or lite editions for download so users can practice their skills before advancing to the complete and more costly versions. I used to buy books on these packages and work through them step by step. Not only are you saving yourself money, but you're learning a new, marketable skill. I can be the editor if my project's budget can't support hiring one. If the distributor asks for new stills for marketing purposes, I can at no cost use Photoshop to tweak images to their specifications. These small things all add up.

Visual effects are often used for pyrotechnics nowadays. Artists can now purchase pre-keyed, high-resolution elements that can be placed in a shot to simulate such action. Muzzle flashes, bullet hits, sparks, glass breaking, fire, smoke, explosions . . . Special-effect technicians can do that work practically, but it can cost a lot more and also take more time on set to rig. And, of course, you only have a limited number of attempts to get things right. Finding an artist to do this

work for you or even teaching yourself can save *a lot* of money.

Finally, once you've exhausted all of those areas, we come to crew and food. See if the crew rates be reduced. Slightly reduced pay rates can add up and might make all the difference. Instead of paying for a catering company, see if there's a friend or family member who likes cooking and might be interested in preparing the production's food for a fraction of the cost. It's time to get a little ruthless . . . If you don't bring that budget under, then there is no film, or you're footing the bill.

WORKING WITH LOCATIONS

If the location is public land, or is managed by the local film office / commission in your area, then you'll need to contact that film office and begin working with them. I've always found them very helpful (if sometimes overzealous), but that's because they have to protect themselves and their clients. You'll need to fill out a few forms about what you're planning on shooting, your locations and filming times, and anything unconventional about your scene. A risk assessment will also have to be filled in, listing all possible shooting hazards to the crew or the public. Once you've provided a copy of your public liability insurance (normally to the sum of $12.5 million

(£10 million)), you can receive a filming permit. Shooting anything that might cause distress or alarm to the public requires notification of the local film office and the police. It doesn't matter that it's only a film or that it's obvious to everyone that you're on a shoot — they need to know. Maybe you have a knife pulled on someone in the scene, or a gun, or a fight takes place. There might be a camera present, but what if the director considers filming an extreme wide from far away, inside a car? That fight is now open for all to see, and there isn't any sign of a film crew. We've had shoots involving a character discreetly pulling a gun on someone in a scene and had to get creative by shooting the gun as an insert in our backyard. There are ways around it.

If you're filming on private land or with permission from a company, you won't need any paperwork from your local film office. If you are filming anything hazardous or potentially alarming to the passing public, inform the local police authority. When you have the all-clear from the location, do two things: First, politely ask for the telephone numbers of all company members involved with the shoot. Second, send a confirmation email or call on the day before shooting. You may have finalized the location and gotten the go-ahead a week or 10 days before, and everything is in place. But people do need

reminding. If the person who gave permission to film at the private boatyard says they will get the yard manager to open up on shooting day, get the boatyard manager's phone number. What if your contact doesn't ask him, or the manager oversleeps? You need a foolproof way of contacting whoever can get things done on the day of the shoot. Also ask if there is anyone else in their company that needs to sign off on your shoot. I've been ambushed by this: The day before we were to shoot, the contact who gave me permission finally consulted with his superior, who pulled the plug! So be prepared.

Whatever location you find yourself shooting, whether privately or publicly arranged through a film office, you'll need public liability insurance. Accidents will and do happen. A crew member swings that lighting stand and takes a big chunk out of the old oak dining table in that mansion house. The heat from that 12-kilowatt light placed too close to the window cracks it . . . You need to cover yourself.

Make sure parking is adequate too. On a larger production, this responsibility falls to the location manager. But until you have the budget to hire one, it's the producer's job. How many parking spaces, and how big? How close are they to the shooting location? Do we need parking permits printed? How many? Is there space at the location that can be used as a green room for talent when they're not filming? Somewhere for hair and make-up to prepare? A room for the camera team to keep their gear safe and secure? And toilet facilities?

Leave the location better than you found it. Put everything back to how it was, take pictures before the shoot if need be, and make sure things are neat, swept up, and in their rightful place. No water bottles left on the shelf, no gaffer tape on the floor, no garbage pails still full. Since you might need to come back for pickups (extra filming days), leave the location neat and tidy and make a good impression for any future filmmakers who might want to use it.

Location databases are a wonderful resource to research too. They list hundreds of locations all over the country, from old runways to mansion houses. They are well worth looking into, but the agency will impose a rental charge.

BUDGETING FOR SET-BUILDING AND STUDIO RENTAL

Your project might be all filmed on location, whether shooting interiors or exteriors. For lower-budget films, this is sometimes the easiest and cheapest approach. Some of your settings, like a science-fiction environment, might not actually exist, or maybe it's a set you need to destroy on camera — in which case you might be constructing that environment as a purpose-built set in a studio.

A studio space could be almost anything, from an empty, disused warehouse to a fully equipped, soundproof stage. If it's an empty warehouse, what power might be needed to run your lights? You might need to bring your own generators if the building is without power. You might hire an established studio to build a set, or use the space for shooting green-screen work. Using the studio option and constructing a set immediately incur costs: materials, set dressings, crews. Here are some things to consider:

- You might need an area for your production designer / set builder to create the set beforehand. Even though the set will be filmed in the studio, it may need to be constructed and prepared elsewhere. Your set designer / construction team might already work in such an area, or you might need to arrange a space yourself. This set will then have to be transported to the studio, perhaps incurring van-rental costs. It might even be more cost effective to hire the studio for longer and have your team build the set where it will be shot.

- You can build your sets from various types of materials that keep costs down. Ask your construction team what is available. Investigate if anyone is finishing up a shoot with set pieces you could buy off them cheaply. You can also reuse sets still standing from previous shoots.

- Bring in the director of photography when designing your sets. They will have ideas on everything from the size of windows to what practical lights could be built into the set. Also speak to the DP about where to position the set within the studio itself. Ideally you're as close to the center of the studio space as possible to allow for the optimal positioning of lights. I've seen sets built very close to the studio walls; the DP was then expected to find room for their lights to shine through the set window.

- Check with the studio rental about electrical costs. This can be a hidden cost that surprises some producers. They assume it comes with the studio rental fee, and are then left a little shaken as a large electricity bill is added to the invoice.

- Allow for build days, pre-lighting, and strike time. Your designers will need between a day and a few weeks to actually build the set in the studio. Then the DP and gaffer will need time to pre-light the set before shooting. Once shooting has wrapped, you'll need time to strike or remove the set from the studio. Ensure you budget for this. Even though you might be shooting for four days, you might need two days to build, one to prelight, and one to strike, making your studio rental eight days, not four.

SANTA AND HIS REINDEER

Here's a bit of a fun exercise to get your producer's brain ticking. Think as creatively and as practically as you can. As a producer, you must *always* have one eye on the budget. What if your script opens with:

EXT. TOWN CENTER — NIGHT

Snow falls as crowds line the streets to see Santa's sleigh and his reindeer land in the town center. Flocks of small children surround the sleigh and pet the reindeer.

As a producer, reading this should have put a hundred thoughts in your head. First, what are the costs and logistics? We have to source the reindeer. And Santa himself (actor + costume). We need the means to feed, house, and clean up after the reindeer. We must close off the road, which means permits, permission from businesses, and traffic management. All this takes place at night, likely necessitating extra heaters, power, and food. Are there young performers? Night work is often hard, so what restrictions must you consider when working with child actors? Where can you keep them all off set, warm and dry, when they are not shooting? How will Santa and his reindeer arrive? Will this be a computer-generated image (CGI) Santa transitioning into the live-action version as he lands? Is the snow a practical on-set effect, or is it CGI? How many people are required to carry out the effects work? The list goes on . . . In the end, the scene might well be set in someone's driveway, during the day, with Santa and the reindeer only heard off screen as adult characters predict it will snow later and they should go tell the kids . . .

MARKETING, STILLS, AND SOCIAL MEDIA

Your film's marketing ideas need to be considered and implemented during development, pre-production, and production, not just during final cut. It really begins when you first announce the film, be it online or in trade magazines. Slowly drip-feeding snippets of information, images, and video can start building your audience.

So what other things should a producer be mindful of in this regard? Firstly, ensure there are an adequate number of stills for the marketing and distribution of the film; still photos are often overlooked or forgotten during shooting. *Every image or asset released in connection with your film must be of the highest standard.* I don't just mean in focus, but the image itself must *say something*. I often see films in production for which the director or producer releases what I term a "non photo." It's a wide shot of the set featuring backs of heads and blurry moving people, eyes caught mid-blink . . . Your stills need to be both technically proficient (well framed, correctly exposed, etc.) and interesting. Is it funny, or does it provoke an emotional reaction? *Every* image represents your film; make them all count. You're communicating the story, quality of the production, and budget, either consciously or subconsciously, with everything you release to promote the film. To add value for other filmmakers you could show and describe a complicated lighting breakdown, or give outsiders an insider's glimpse of the film industry.

I advise getting at least fifty high-resolution stills of the onscreen action, and fifty of the behind-the-scenes / filming process. These might be for your own benefit, or for posters, film festivals, social media, DVD / Blu-ray covers, or distribution. The onscreen action stills could at a push be taken as screengrabs from the graded image in the edit, but the quality might not be as high as distributors like — so your still photographer should take some.

Behind-the-scenes action stills need to "tell the story" of the film being produced; they're not just random photographs of what went on behind the camera. For example, we might see the actor with clapperboard in front of them and a camera in front of that, a nearby light illuminating the scene. Anyone not privy to the filmmaking process would see this image deconstructed and learn its design. You might also get a few shots of the director talking to the actors, and a well-lit shot of the studio set. A still photographer has a specific work-driven purpose; taking random, fun pictures or establishing continuity is not part of their job description. I've been on sets where a talented still photographer was hired, but they specialized in landscapes or portraits. Their technical ability isn't the issue; it's knowing what images need to be taken.

Social media has pervaded every part of our lives. Don't deduce that *not* releasing content may somehow keep things mysterious, and that you're generating buzz by your absence, leaving people guessing and wondering what's coming. No

one cares, as unfortunately, you're not Marvel or *Star Wars* just yet. Drip-feeding content from the start of production is the best way, slowly building your audience and making them aware. The value of an image is worth more in the moment, slowly getting more exposure than had it been kept locked away and used as part of a mass release of images a week prior to release.

Besides still images, you'll also need to cut a trailer. It must really shine and sell your film, whether a distribution company is preparing it for you or (more) likely you're cutting one yourself. Every shot and every cut matters, just like in the finished film. And just like in the finished film, the most important thing is . . . story! You might only need one line or two to set it up, but the audience needs to know what the story is, and fast. Then you can cut in all the action, special effects, stunts, and money shots you like. Even the trailer must give us something about story, concept, and conflict between characters, and should have a beginning, middle, and end. *A good trailer, at its core, asks a question the audience needs answered — so much so that they see the movie.* A film offers ninety minutes to sensibly place all these elements, but the trailer affords but two. What's the premise? What's at stake? You might have one chance to get your audience's interest, so make it count.

CHAPTER 3

CASTING YOUR BLOCKBUSTER

"The greatest mistake a young director can make is to want to show the actor what to do. It's like asking an artist to design a poster but sketching it for him. An actor is a performer."

— JEAN-PIERRE JEUNET, DIRECTOR

Casting can make or break your film. It can be a long and laborious process, but once complete, 90% of the director's job is done. If your budget allows, perhaps hire a casting agency to read your script and offer a list of potential candidates for the roles. If your budget is tight you will have to conduct your own search, scouring the film and acting communities for talented thespians. Your cast could come from local theater productions, online notices and callouts, friends of friends, talent agencies, previous films you may have seen, or actors you already know well. Finding the right actor to fit your character can be very hard, but the excitement when you've

done so justifies the process. Casting the lead roles is very important, but casting minor parts requires equal focus. Your whole scene or film could rest on the weakest link. If you have three talented performers in a scene spitting out your witty dialogue, only to have a minor character with one line mess the whole thing up, the scene will fall apart.

There are many acting websites that list actors for producers and directors to pore over. These pages will give all the relevant physical descriptions and abilities: height, size, eye color, hair, experience, skills, as well as photos and a video showreel. Their CV or résumé will list what TV, film, theater, and radio work they've done, too. Once you have contacted an actor, or they have gotten in touch with you about your production, it will be time to arrange an audition.

AUDITIONS

Auditions can be great fun. You're meeting new people, and you could receive some new ideas and insights about the script. To begin with, talk to your actors about things not related to the work. How they got here, the weather, anything to give them a chance to relax and you an opportunity to get to know them as a person. Video the auditions so you and other members of the production team can review them later, but let actors know they're being recorded. Have a few spare copies of the script with you. If other actors have been cast or you know some who are free, take them to the auditions to read with the new people. Scenes can go flat pretty quickly with an untrained actor, most probably the producer, trying to read with the trained actors . . .

If you send an actor their script before the day of the audition, highlight a few scenes that enable them to show you a range of different emotions and transitions. This could be the big confrontation scene, or the one depicting the woman's husband leaving her — a meaty exchange to

give the cast something to work with. Let them know that they have the opportunity to read more than once, as it might take a moment to get into the zone. It's all about creating a relaxed and calm environment to elicit the best performances. Take the pressure off by giving your actors space. No one likes the cold, hard director who thinks keeping people on edge produces the best work . . .

Try not to tell them what you expect, or how you want them to play the scene, either. Let them *show* you what they've prepared. They want you to know what they can do, which might be precisely what you were planning to suggest! Once they've shown you what they've prepared, give them some direction and ask them to play the scene differently. It doesn't have to be the way you see the scene playing on film, but by asking for something new, you are ascertaining whether they can take direction. They might be wonderful in the part they performed, but can they adapt and change to new approaches when on set?

Do they know their lines? This is a biggie! Allowances can be made if scripts are being sent out to actors late, but how much you permit is up to you. Most of the talented professional actors I've had the pleasure of working with have known their lines no matter how late the script was received, even if this was the night before! They changed plans or stayed up late, whatever was required to know the text well enough to perform the following day. I've seen auditions where actors promise to know the text well come shooting day even though they are unprepared at that moment. On the day of the shoot, guess what? They don't know their lines! The writing may be on the wall regarding someone's behavior and attitude early on if you know how to look for it. Ignore this at your peril!

You might also get the actor to improvise around one of the scripted scenes. Maybe they could play an extra scene that is related to the one they've learned. For example, in the script, the character might have just been fired from his or her job. They might not have a husband or wife in the film, but you could improvise a scene where they go home and tell their spouse about losing their job. This would show you other skills of theirs and their understanding of the character. And if they don't know all their lines for the other scene, now they have an opportunity to not be enslaved to them.

If an actor is late for rehearsals, then start without him or her. Most respect the process and will be on time; it could well be a one-off occurrence. But now they know the show goes on without them and that they're not the center of the production.

RELAXED ACTORS AND A RELAXED SET

It pays to have a relaxed set, and the environment on set filters down from the director. He or she dictates the pace and mood on the floor. If the director isn't relaxed, it's normally due to lack of preparation. I've never understood the philosophy of having tension on set, as though this injects some sort of buzz into the performances. Perhaps the actor's last performance was well received and was filmed on a tense set, so they attribute the outcome to this. Relaxation is key here, and this applies to both director and actor. If the actor is relaxed, they are free to try new things and give their best possible performance, and I would encourage you to let them know they can. It's okay to move out of their comfort zone.

STANISLAVSKY AND THE GIVEN CIRCUMSTANCES

Constantin Stanislavsky was a Russian actor, director, and teacher born in 1863. He changed the way a lot of actors approached their craft by developing new methods of working. Stanislavsky spoke of the "Given Circumstances." The Given Circumstances refer to everything that the character has ever done, their physical form, where they are mentally, and their current environment. If our main character hates water after a near-death experience, and someone suggests going on a boat, this character will react accordingly. If Character A is about to go on a long road trip with friends, and finds their enemy Character B in the car, they'll deliver their lines with appropriate enmity.

Emotion comes out of both Given Circumstances and action played in the moment. It's worth noting here how little work the actor really has to do. The audience knows the character's circumstances and can probably anticipate how they will react. The actor's "reaction" or line doesn't require the Given Circumstances to be embedded within it, or that it be used to telegraph their thoughts to audience. The trick is to let the audience and camera do most of your work for you. That's good acting!

"MAGIC AS-IF" AND BEHAVIOR

I first read about using "magic as-if" in Judith Weston's excellent book *Directing Actors*. As-if is a tool to elicit earthier performances and make small adjustments or tweaks to actors' choices. The as-if doesn't have any direct relation to the scene in question; what you're after is the result of the associated behavior.

In a World War II film I made for ITV television, a soldier and a young war widow dance at a Christmas party. The woman has not been close to a man since her husband died in battle. The young solider approaches the widow and propositions her, to which she agrees; he takes her hand and walks to the dancefloor. The scene wasn't quite working and lacked the emotional significance I sought, so I told the actor portraying the soldier to act *"as if* her bones were made of glass." His behavior now changed. He gently offered his hand to the widow and guided her to the dancefloor, keeping a slight distance (to not scare her) and supporting her all the way. The direction resulted in a behavior that now showed us how emotionally fragile she was and that he needed to treat her the same way physically. As-ifs are slightly abstract, but help convey feeling and direction to the actor.

Behavior is perhaps the most important thing an actor and director need to fine-tune. *It is all about what the camera sees.* Any thinking or process the actor participates in must result in a behavior; it has to be physical so the camera can film it. So don't tell your actors what their characters are thinking, tell them what to do; any instructions from you as a director should result in or a change of behavior.

There is a scene in Steven Spielberg's *Close Encounters of the*

Third Kind (1977) where a 5-year-old boy had to react to seeing an alien off camera. Spielberg needed looks of wonder and surprise and a few gradations in between. To direct the young actor traditionally by telling him to look surprised and in awe might have provided mixed results. Instead, Spielberg dressed up the boy's make-up artist in a gorilla suit and placed them behind the camera. Later in the scene, the make-up artist removed the gorilla mask so the boy saw it was actually a friendly face underneath messing around, and the child's expression changed accordingly. He displayed the joy, wonder, and surprise needed for the take. Now, I'm not saying dress up in a gorilla suit or go to bizarre lengths to motivate your actors, but what can we learn about directing and behavior? You need to trust your adult actor to deliver his or her performance, and

making them angry or uncomfortable on set to provoke their character may not be the way to go. Whatever process you choose, only the end result matters. The audience doesn't care how you get there.

Actor behavior will change and adapt as new information arrives in a scene. An actor could stop drinking, turn their head, or open their mouth — anything physical to demonstrate how they feel. Seek out an action or piece of business that shows they've received new information. Hearing the information with no visible change in behavior is as good as no information. Imagine if a character picks up the phone and receives bad news. If we don't hear the other person talking, how could we show the bad news? If the character picked up the phone with a somewhat neutral expression, it might be hard to gauge their response to what they're hearing. However, if

3.1. Cary Guffey in *Close Encounters of the Third Kind* (1977).

they picked up the phone still smiling from a previous conversation, the story is told when their expression changes and the smile slowly fades. It's all about characters' behavior.

I've used looks and glances from different scenes, some shot *after* I've called cut, and even included footage filmed between takes. They weren't necessarily thinking about the scene at hand, but a look they gave the other actor was perfect for a reaction shot elsewhere. I cut that look in to magically get the perfect performance.

Intellectual chitchat between an actor and director can lead to "paralysis by analysis." Too much thinking! Actors have been cast because they have the looks, qualities, and talents you want for your roles. Some actors may feel unprepared without this extra discussion work. Pack what you need to go on vacation; there's no need to bring your entire wardrobe.

All good screen actors know how little they actually have to do. They know the audience will project the exact amount of emotion needed onto their blank canvas, validating their performance. In his book *On Directing Film*, filmmaker and author David Mamet gives a wonderful example of two animals in the forest. Cutting together a shot of a bird eating a worm and looking up with a shot of a deer walking and stopping to look up suggests "danger in the forest." The director doesn't need to talk at length

with the bird about how he hasn't eaten for days and when to glance up and look scared. The movement and juxtaposition of the two images tell that story. To add to it would be overkill.

If your actor is doing it right, don't meddle! Let them be. Don't feel the need to direct too much; it can mess things up. If the scene calls for an actor to walk down a corridor and open a door, that's it. The actor, if they've done their homework, knows what has happened in the previous scene, so they work that in. They need a gentle reminder, but not much.

ACTION VERBS

Action verbs are a wonderful tool that not only can be used for directing your actors but also motivating and inspiring them. Let's say one character is asking another to stay in a relationship and not leave their marriage. Maybe you start with the verb *convince* to get them to stay, but you want more volume and intensity. You could *plead* with them to stay, or raise the stakes further and *beg* them to stay. Conversely, maybe your scene involves a character asking questions of another; they're overdoing it and coming at the scene a little hard, so you ask them to *quiz* the other character rather than *interrogate* them.

Action verbs enable an actor to focus exclusively on the other actor in a scene. It stops them from thinking about themselves, if they're good enough, or if their good side is being spotlighted. The whole scene strengthens when each actor's attention is on the other performer. Verbs help the actor play their character's want or objective with an emotional center, which is what you want. Other verbs you might find useful include: instruct, intimidate, confront, suffocate, seduce, appease, inform, attack. As a director, part of your homework can be to go through the script and label what verb or verbs each character might be playing. It might be one per scene, or maybe two or three. Then when in rehearsal or on set, you can give that clear direction to your actor. Keep it simple, though; don't fall into the trap of giving a verb for each of the 25 lines in the scene! Each verb will cover a series of lines until the scene changes gear.

PLAYING THE PRIORITY — ACTORS AND ACTION

An actor can't play more than one thing at once. There may be a lot going on in a film, but a character's primary "want" will generally be front and center in their minds. A good way of determining what to focus on is to always play the priority. What is the most important thing for your character at that moment? Then play that. Yes, your wife has left you and you've lost your job — but if you're then in a car accident with your daughter, play the car accident. The character's primary focus is the accident. Is their daughter okay? Can they move her? If she's okay, can they get to their phone to call an ambulance? They can't play the car accident *while* feeling sorry for themselves over their wife leaving. Making sure the actor plays the priority maintains authenticity, the greatest good a director can pursue.

If the stage directions in the script read: "Karen is happy that she's won the lottery, but a little sad her dog died," how can the actor play that? Directors will sometimes give actors similarly mixed, unplayable directions, and it can be confusing for actors to know what to do. In trying to play both elements and muddle the two, what is performed is a mixed bag that doesn't satisfy either notion. Always play the priority.

CHAPTER 4

FILMING YOUR BLOCKBUSTER

*"All of one's experience of life subconsciously informs
every creative decision one makes. That's what makes
each individual cinematographer different."*
— JANUSZ KAMINSKI, ASC, CINEMATOGRAPHER

So you've got your script, cast your talent, booked your locations, and now you need to get this blockbuster in the can! Before we roll, let's look at aspects of the camera and lighting and what we can do to add lots of production value to your film.

Regarding lighting, there is more to cinematography than beautiful images. If the audience notices your "beautiful" photography, you've failed. The film's images should help them get swept up in the story, not bring them out of it by making them consciously aware. Each film demands its own look and feel. So your images must be appropriate for the story at that particular moment in time. If they happen to be beautiful and appropriate, then all well and good.

PREPARATION

Some of the preparation that a director of photography (DP) does will merge with the work that the director is doing. They're both thinking about shots, angles, and how best to tell the story. Preparation is the key to confidence when you're working: know the material and the tone of the film, and make sure you're on the same page as the director. Before you go on location recces (pre-filming visits to locations to determine their suitability for shooting), or think about what lights and new gear you'll use, the script must be solid and ready to shoot. Reading the script should give you an idea of the tone and feel of the piece, and the emotions being portrayed. The subject matter, settings, characters, and action will all help suggest how it should be photographed. Decisions as to whether the lighting should be high-key or low-key, or if the camera is handheld or filmed more rigidly on a dolly or tripod, can then be made with the director. Take your cues from the script, and don't arbitrarily imbue them with unrelated looks or styles.

The director will draw up a shot list to show the director of photography what they have in mind. They can then work together on tweaking and adjusting shots to help tell the story.

As part of the DP's preparation, they break down the script to note what scenes are day or night, and what time of day it is. They will also draw up any lighting diagrams or schematics blocking out light placement. These can be useful guides for the gaffer and electrical department. The DP will also be having discussions on style, referencing any relevant images or film material. The color palette of the sets and actors' costumes will all contribute to how the image will look on screen, necessitating conversations with the production designer and costume supervisor.

LOCATION RECCES

As a DP, what are your main points of interest on a recce? You need to look at how much space is available to you on location. Is there enough space for your dollies, lights, and crew? It might work visually, but can it be done practically? If you are lighting from outside the windows, is there enough space to put your lights? If you're on the second floor of a building, or working around the location owner's prized flowerbed, lights might be an issue. Access to power is also a major consideration. If you're filming in a private residence, get permission from the homeowner to use their electricity. If you're in an old abandoned warehouse or a similar location, your options might be natural light, battery-operated lights, or using your own generator for power. If there is a power source but only one inconveniently located electrical socket, add lots of extension cables to your equipment list. All these things need to be considered beforehand. You don't want your unpreparedness to cause trouble on the day of shooting.

If possible, visit the location at different times of the day or week, but definitely at the time of day you plan to shoot. Yes, it might be quiet now, but what about the day of the week you're shooting, or the time you're shooting? Where the sun will be at certain times is also worth noting. If you're filming someone walking down a road, you might find that from 4 pm onward the sun shines directly down that road behind your actor, and now all your characters will be wonderfully backlit. You may now apply this information to your schedule. There are many phone apps that give the position of the sun at any given time. I use them on location recces to find out where the sun will be when we plan to film. Tiny details that all prepare you for the shoot.

LENSING THE ACTION — PRIMES OR ZOOMS?

The camera equipment you rent to shoot your blockbuster may include either prime or zoom lenses. Primes are fixed focus length lenses that come in various sizes. A standard set might consist of 18 mm, 25 mm, 32 mm, 40 mm, 50 mm, 85 mm, 100 mm, and 135 mm. If you want to go in tighter on the action, or frame your shot wider using a prime lens, either change the lens or pick up your camera and physically move forward or back. A zoom lens has a varying focal length and enables you to change the shot size by zooming in or zooming out of the action. Zoom lenses also come in various focal lengths from 16 mm–35 mm, 24 mm–105 mm, 70 mm–200 mm, 19 mm–90 mm, and 24 mm–240 mm. Some zooms are so large and

heavy that their tripods require additional support.

Top Hollywood cinematographers Roger Deakins (*Skyfall, The Shawshank Redemption, No Country for Old Men*) and John Seale (*Prince of Persia, The Perfect Storm, Dead Poets Society*) differ greatly on the use of prime and zoom lenses. No one filmmaker or method is correct, and everyone has their own way of shooting things. In the excellent book *Cinematography for Directors* by Jacqueline B. Frost, Deakins says, "I rarely have a zoom in the kit. I don't like to use zooms; I work with prime lenses all the time." Seale, on the other hand, loves the flexibility and freedom of zooms, and argues that there used to be an issue with quality between primes and zooms that better manufacturing has rendered moot. "I always use zooms. I don't use primes. Some of the boys say, 'But the zoom lens doesn't have the quality,' and I say, 'Yeah, but it's consistent.' If that's the look of the film all the way through, the audience will get over it in the first three shots [even] if it's not as sharp as they're used to."

Having worked with both types, there is a nice quality to primes, which allow you the discipline of choosing a shot size and sticking to it. Also, using primes when learning cinematography will give you a much better understanding of focal lengths and the different looks achievable with them. But most of the time, the perfect frame composition might require a slight zoom in or zoom out to frame out an object or person appearing on the side of the shot. To make those adjustments by turning a barrel can save a lot of time, especially when shooting action sequences. Often a second shot presents itself while filming the first one. Filming on a zoom lens allows you the flexibility to quickly punch in and grab more footage. To do this on primes would require changing a lens or physically picking up the camera and moving. This adds up to one or two minutes minimum, which over the course of the day could cost you shots, time, or both. You can also use the zoom as a tool. Shots zooming the action closer into frame, i.e., showing the image get bigger on camera, are rare these days. They connote bad 1970s television or poor-quality movies, but you can use them to subtly change the frame size during a pan or a dolly shot. The shot changes to have the desired impact, but the audience didn't see the zoom.

When shooting any sort of action scene, I like the flexibility that zooms offer. Actors and action are moving, and so is the camera — so I need to be able adjust on the fly.

DEPTH OF FIELD

Depth of field refers to the points in your shot that are nearest to and farthest from the camera that look sharp and in focus. If you shoot with a fairly high f-stop, say, f/8 or f/11, and focus on your subject, your subject and the background will both appear clearly. For more of the background to look out of focus, open your aperture to something like f/2.8. Some DPs like to shoot what is called "wide open," which is having the lowest f-stop possible, maybe f/1.4 or f/2.

Some DPs like to shoot what is called "wide open," which is having the widest f-stop possible, maybe f/1.4 or f/2. This means a lot of the image behind your subject is out of focus, which guides the audience where to look. But there are advantages: these images have a very pleasing look, and make the audience feel like they are watching something a little more "expensive." Having a shallow depth of field is commonly associated with bigger-budget productions or Hollywood movies. A shallow depth of field can both make your images look more expensive and help the audience embrace your story. Shooting around f/4 enables the background to be a little soft while still seeing the surroundings, offering the audience a sense of place, and giving the focus puller a better chance of keeping things sharp.

A single shot with a shallow depth of field taken in isolation might look very good, but you risk the scene's sense of place disappearing. Lengthy edits of shots with a shallow focus may cause the audience to lose their orientation since they are being deprived of a background for a long time. Some designers regularly create lovely sets that are seldom seen on screen since they were filmed in soft focus. There is more to photography than a shallow depth of field.

Maintain a fairly large depth of field when shooting action scenes; you don't want to miss any action because you're out of focus. Things can happen fast on screen. You want to be prepared and give yourself the best possible chance of capturing events as they unfold.

ASPECT RATIO

Aspect ratio refers to the height and width of the frame. It is presently numerically with two numbers separated by a colon. We have 1.33:1 (or 4:3), 1.77:1 (or 16:9), 1.85:1, and 2.39:1. The first number gives you the width of the image, and the second gives you the height.

What shooting ratio you choose for your blockbuster is a decision for the director, director of photography,

and producer, factoring in the script, aesthetics, location, and budget. 16:9 is the universal format for digital video and some filmmakers use it, or choose this ratio but frame and later crop it in post-production for 2.39:1. Whatever frame size you choose, it must enhance and benefit the story being told. The widescreen ratio of 2.39:1 can be used by shooting a 16:9 frame and masking in post-production, or by using a 4:3 sensor and 2x anamorphic lenses to fill the whole width and height of the image. Anamorphic lenses squeeze the image vertically during recording, though it is later un-squeezed when being displayed or projected, thus using the entire frame rather than masking parts in post-production. Anamorphic has an advantage: it uses all of the image sensor or film negative rather than cropping it to arrive at the ratio of choice. There is also a slight decrease in depth of field due to the amount of glass in the lenses.

Traditionally, ratios of 1.85:1, 1.77:1, or 16:9 are used for more drama-based stories, and a larger frame of 2.39:1 is used to shoot epic landscapes or more spectacular

4.1. The main aspect ratios.

films of a wider scope. 2.39:1 is not the be-all and end-all of blockbuster cinema, though. It is used by a lot of larger-than-life films, but sometimes subject matter and location warrant a taller frame to best tell the story. The original *Star Wars* trilogy (1977, 1980, 1983) used the 2:39.1 ratio, as the stories featured long spaceships and epic battles. *Jurassic Park* (1993) had tall dinosaurs, so Spielberg and his DP, Dean Cundey, ASC, chose the taller 1.85:1 format. Blockbusters *Robin Hood: Prince of Thieves* (1991) and *Predator* (1987) are both action films whose stories feature lots of tall trees, so the filmmakers framed in 1.85:1. *Titanic* (1997) featured a long ship sailing the ocean, so 2.39:1 was chosen by James Cameron and his DP, Russell Carpenter, ASC.

However, times are changing; 2.39:1 is now being used for genres like romantic comedy and period drama. Consider this quote from *American*

Cinematographer magazine: "In 1990, 80 percent of theatrical wide releases in the U.S. were in the 1.85:1 aspect ratio. In 2010, only 29 percent were 1.85:1. In those two decades, there was a clear straight-line decline in 1.85:1 movies and an equal straight-line increase in 2.39:1 movies. In 2016, 71 percent of theatrical releases in the U.S. were 2.39:1, 20 percent were 1.85:1, and 9 percent were 'other' aspect ratios, including 1.78:1 and even the traditional Academy aspect ratio of 1.37:1."

The *Lethal Weapon* series featured an interesting choice of aspect ratios. Director Richard Donner and DP Stephen Goldblatt, ASC, BSC, chose to shoot the first film in 1.85:1 as the story was intimate and character based. When the sequel came along in 1989, with bigger characters and more action, the lost intimacy inspired a ratio change, now opting for the wider 2.39:1 frame.

4.2. *Lethal Weapon 2* (1989) and subsequent sequels switched to a 2.39:1 aspect ratio.

Some filmmakers choose to shoot 2.39:1 simply because it is commonly associated with more expensive-looking productions. The story and content of the film are not considered. Every filmmaker has their reasons, but when choosing your aspect ratio, first look at the story, the location, and most importantly, ask what feels right for the film that you're making.

COMPOSITION

Composition is the frame. Everything that you see or don't see within your shot. Composition is a very important part of cinematography; use it to tell your story. The Rule of Thirds is a compositional tool camera operators use to align their images. Early painters and still photographers used it before filmmakers adopted it. By dividing the frame into thirds by using two vertical and horizontal lines in the mind's eye, the operator simply positions objects, people, or locations on those lines. Placing these things on the lines looks good, but having objects or people positioned where the lines cross is even better. Check out this still from *Jurassic Park* (1993) to see this composition in action. The jeep and the *T. rex*'s feet are all positioned in the bottom third. The *T. rex*'s mouth is where the left third and the top third cross, and Sam Neill's Alan Grant character is positioned in the right third.

Using the Rule of Thirds and adjusting the composition of the frame can make your images look a lot better. Take a look at this shot of

4.3. Rule of Thirds in action over a shot from *Jurassic Park* (1993).

4.4. Rule of Thirds in action during a close-up of Naomie Harris in *Skyfall* (2012).

Naomie Harris as Moneypenny in *Skyfall* (2012).

In the close-up we see the head is positioned on the right third, and the eyes are where the top third meets the right third as well. To get the eyes on the top third, the top of the head is cut off. This is okay! Some people think you need to see the whole of the head, but you don't. A close-up is for the eyes, so first ensure they're well composed in the frame. A good close-up cuts off at the hairline and moves down to the bottom of the neckline. If the actor moves and their eyes move off that third, the camera should move with them. A tiny movement of the head to look down at something requires the operator to tilt the camera down too. If not, the result will be the actor's chin touching the bottom of (or moving out of) the frame. This is a very important skill for the camera operator to have. Your eye should be constantly scanning the frame to keep the composition, and if you sense an actor is about to move, be ready to adjust and compensate.

This framing device makes the audience feel comfortable. There is enough space around the character to breathe and move, and the audience knows where everything is. The trick is to know when to break these rules.

Break the Rule of Thirds to suit your own compositional desires. Some recent film and TV work regularly deviates from convention to give the frames a more artistic look or abstract feel. All acceptable if that's what you want. You can also break the thirds convention for effect, inducing an uneasy feeling in the audience to reflect your character's emotional state. A compromised frame like this makes the audience feel off-kilter or creates a sense of apprehension, which can be used to good effect. Check out this shot from

4.5. In *The Outlaw Josey Wales* (1976), Clint Eastwood uses a compromised frame to show his grief.

the Clint Eastwood film *The Outlaw Josey Wales* (1976). When Eastwood buries his son, his emotional turmoil is reflected in his positioning in the frame.

Look at the next example of the Rule of Thirds being broken in Matt Reeves's monster movie *Cloverfield* (2008). Supposedly filmed by amateurs on a handheld camera, all of the framing is purposely poorly composed. Never once do the characters or monster appear in frame in a well-composed shot, as per professional standards. It's a great tool to master so you know when to break it.

When shooting action or a chase with a moving or handheld camera, keeping the composition looking good can be tricky. Avoid heads being cut off the top of the frame, or having too much headspace. Sometimes you have a good first and last frame, but the material in between, where the subject is moving, is not really usable. Try filming someone

4.6. Screenshot of *Cloverfield* (2008) demonstrating how the Rule of Thirds can be broken for effect.

moving unrehearsed. Observe their body language to see if they're about to turn a corner or stop and change direction. You don't want to be chasing a perfect frame until they stop.

OVER-THE-SHOULDER SHOTS

Whether you decide to frame your characters clean (without anyone in the foreground) or shoot over-the-shoulder (OTS) of other actors comes down to your personal taste and your characters' relationships. With the camera literally placed over the shoulder, we see what the character sees, be it another person, object, or location. The audience knows they are in the character's point of view. OTS shots also let us know that someone is listening to what is being said since we can literally see the listener's ear in frame. They also aid geography, and we get a sense of how far away the other person or object is. They are a powerful framing device.

An out-of-focus foreground element can look pleasing to the eye and create a sense of depth. Exercise care with OTS shots if the wide shot has established a character as being up against a wall, couch, or similar prop. You might "cheat" your actors forward in order to frame your OTS shot, but then it might look like the camera is literally positioned inside the wall or couch! Either that, or the characters have suddenly sprung forward since the viewer subconsciously knows that wall didn't move. I think audiences are aware of perspective, even if they don't consciously know it. The audience knows there is a wall in the scene, so don't complicate your setups or confuse the audience by trying to make your OTS shot work in these circumstances. Shoot a clean shot of the actor instead.

Over-the-shoulder shots can be a wonderful storytelling tool too. Look at this shot of Bonnie Bedelia in *Die Hard* (1988). Bruce Willis's John McClane character's imposing shoulder almost

4.7. Bruce Willis as John McClane in *Die Hard* (1988) dominates the frame in this over-the-shoulder shot.

fills the frame, pushing down on his wife as they argue. The scene would have work perfectly fine were it composed more conventionally, but altering the frame and composition like this is good storytelling.

BLOCKING THE SCENE AND SHOOTING ORDER

Blocking the action on screen is an important part of creating and shooting great images. Blocking refers to the staging of a scene — determining the actors' positioning and movements — implemented by the director, director of photography, and actors. The director and DP then establish where the camera can go and what coverage / angles are required to best capture the action. It is a compromise between these three parties, since the character's actions and motivations need to be justifiable and also read well on camera. Staging an actor standing by a window so they get good light might be ideal for the DP, but the actor thinks the character should be sitting by the bed. If the actor's positioning works well for both the DP and the actor, you have a winner. As a director and a DP, I've asked actors how they feel about turning around or moving to the doorway to make a scene play better on camera. If they can justify the action with what they believe the character would do,

it produces a better scene visually and keeps the actor comfortable and involved in developing the sequence. We will cover depth and lighting shortly in more detail, but when blocking, maintain a sense of depth to the scene by keeping actors and action away from the walls. Also make sure the camera is on the fill side (opposite the key light) of the actor's face; the ensuing light wrap is very complimentary to your cast. If the actor can say their lines and move around the set, and I'm able to keep them keyed on the opposite side of the camera, I'm visually satisfied.

Blocking the scene would work as part of the rehearsal and shooting order. Make sure you block the whole scene being filmed, not just part of it, lest a subsequent surprise derail your shot. Work with the first assistant director (1st AD) and/or director, to stage and plan the shot in this order:

- Clear all crew and block the shot / scene with the actors and key heads of department.
- Once blocked, clear all cast and crew from the set and give space and time for the lighting team to rig and place their lights to shoot the scene. (Use stand-ins instead of the actors if need be.)
- Call the actors back, rehearse for the camera, and tweak if necessary.
- Shoot.

Once the shot is in the can, this process is then repeated until the day's work is done. It's good practice to clear the set to allow the DP and the lighting team room to move and light the scene. It makes work very difficult if cast and crew are standing around talking while the DP, gaffer, and the electrical department are positioning stands, lighting, and laying cables in the same space.

CAMERA PLACEMENT

Perhaps one of the most important factors in cinematography is camera placement. After blocking the scene with the director and actors, finding the best place to put the camera is paramount. For me, this has become fairly instinctual; what feels right will rise to the surface and present itself. Do not arbitrarily force a shot position onto the scene. Going Dutch (having the camera at an angle) or having a high shot just because you think it looks cool or you haven't used that type of shot for a while might damage your storytelling. If the scene involves your actor crying, you might want to be in front of them and in close. Maybe the character is very shy and generally hides her feelings, so you shoot behind her and eventually have her turn toward camera. What works best for the story? Cinematographers factor in their lights and light sources

when formulating camera placement. If the camera placement fits the story appropriately, and ticks the boxes visually by keeping the depth of your location and enabling you to shoot your actor on the fill / shadow side of their face, you may have found the perfect spot.

The height of the camera is also an important factor to consider. Most things that we experience on a day-to-day basis happen at normal eye level. If you position the camera in a higher or lower place, have a good reason for it. Like many examples here, these different techniques are best done subtly. Maybe you are filming the President giving a speech, or a bully in a playground. You could position the camera just below eye level to suggest the power wielded by the President, or an intimidation tactic by the bully. The opposite might also be true. Maybe as a couple argues on the stairs of their mansion, the man is filmed from a slightly higher angle, looking down on him to suggest he is either in the wrong or is of lower status in the relationship. Subtle is the keyword here.

WHEN AND WHY SHOULD YOU MOVE THE CAMERA?

Moving your camera during a shot should always be a motivated choice. Ask why you are moving. A camera in motion can establish pace, signify

4.8. Dynamic dolly shots and composition in the action film *Con Air* (1997).

a change in a character's mindset, or make a shot more dynamic and interesting. Take a look at the above still from action film *Con Air* (1997). A low-angle dolly move into John Malkovich keeps the action dynamic and larger than life as the prisoners are being introduced.

Your camera should always have a reason for moving. If it doesn't, it might not reflect the action on screen, the mindset of the characters, or the proper context. I've seen directors stick the camera on a dolly whizzing back and forth, though this would be jarring in a slow, intimate scene. Just because you can move the camera doesn't mean that you should. Move the camera based on intuition and what feels right.

Here's director Sydney Pollack on his approach and reasoning when shooting his lawyer / mobster film *The Firm* (1993): "I decided on this film that no shot would be still. On every shot of every scene, cameraman John Seale had his hand on the zoom or on the head of the tripod, and he would move the camera a bit. It's almost imperceptible, and he did it slowly so you only notice it if you're looking for it. But I think it creates a feeling of instability that was necessary for the story."

Camera movement can be motivated by a character's physical action and their emotional state. Maybe as a character figures something out or realises what has to be done, the camera can slowly push in on their face to help signify this. You can also cut on a camera movement. This wasn't always standard practice, though. A previous generation of editors uniformly waited for the camera to stop moving before cutting away, believing that doing otherwise would unsettle the audience. If done incorrectly, this can be the case. But if executed with the right material and with the camera moving at the appropriate speed, it works.

What types of camera movement are there? There are many, all executed using different pieces of equipment. In essence, if it is moving, it should be the right camera move, with the right piece of equipment, for the right time in the story. My first point is therefore: *the camera doesn't have to move*. Your audience will be distracted if the camera is moving but the story doesn't warrant it. A camera move is a change of perspective. We move to get a different look at something, or to emphasize a point. In my student days, my friends and I were heavily influenced by the big 1980s directors and their moving cameras; they weren't good if they didn't move the camera! Or so we thought. If we had a sequence featuring a character walking to a bus stop, we would shoot a wide, a handheld over-the-shoulder, a close-up of their feet walking and coming to a stop, and a 360º spin as they looked for the bus. Phew, dizzying times! On reflection, a static wide of the bus stop would have sufficed. Maybe a pan along the street to reveal the bus stop, but that's about it. Sometimes the best place for the camera is at eye level, static and just recording the action.

From an aesthetic point of view, moving the camera during a longer wide shot can prove more valuable. The shot is kept alive and made more dynamic and interesting through the slight change in perspective. You'll be less inclined to cut away from it too. The action obviously influences the pace and quality of the movement. Wide shots can be a little flat. Other shots like close-ups highlight facial nuances, contain a shallow depth of field, and generally look pleasing to the eye. If you were shooting on a zoom lens, you could also change the angle a little during the wide shot by either punching in a little tighter or popping a little wider. Then if the editor decides to cut back to it at any point, he or she has a different size shot to use, something new for the audience.

Let's look at what camera movements are available to us, what they might be used for, and what they mean for the action.

- Pan
- Tilt
- Dolly
- Handheld
- Crane
- Steadicam / gimbal
- Aerial / drone

PAN:
The panning shot is where the camera body physically stays in the same position, but looks from right to left or left to right. A good use might be a location where one shot might not take in all the surroundings, so

you pan the camera in order to see everything. Or maybe you're panning with your actor as they walk along the other side of the street.

TILT:

A tilt is the opposite of a pan. Again the camera stays in one place, but this time looks up and down.

DOLLY:

Dollies come in a few forms. The more elaborate (read: expensive) ones have two seats for the cameraperson and focus puller, and smooth air-pressure systems to add vertical moves. The more basic form is a "flatbed" dolly: a flat base on wheels on which you

can place your tripod. Dollies are a great way to add some production value to your piece, and can be very dramatic and subtle. Here's a good tip: To do a dolly move into an actor's close-up for emphasis, set the dolly track at a slight angle to your subject (rather than in a direct line in front of them). This way the camera operator has to adjust a little more during the dolly move, causing the background to change. This change in visual space can make a shot a little more dynamic.

HANDHELD:

Handheld means physically holding the camera rather than using a tripod. Some people like this look, some hate it. If done too much, it can be nauseating. Done right, it can imbue a scene with apprehension and tension. Handheld doesn't mean shaking the camera all over the place, only that the shot is not static. There's a gentle "breathing" to the shot as the camera operator holds it steady. The connotation with handheld is that the camera doesn't quite know what will happen next. There's a documentary and realistic feel to the scene unfolding before you. However, it can also give a low-budget, amateurish feel to the piece if done badly. So it must be used, like any shot and style, in the right place and at the right time. It can also be jarring if you cut between handheld and static shots, so consider how they might cut together.

4.9. A dolly in action.

As a camera operator, finding compositions on the fly can be liberating too, and is quite freeing for the actors since they know that they can be a little off their marks and still have the operator catch them. Camera rental companies can hire "moose bars" for handheld work too. Moose bars are handles that can be attached to the matte box rails under the camera so the operator can hold the camera comfortably and be able to move freely.

It's important to keep an eye on the frame at all times during your handheld shot. Scan the frame constantly for composition, keeping the headroom and onscreen items constant. You want every second to be usable, and you don't want to force the editor to cut away because the middle of a shot isn't good. Shots can start off with a good frame, but as actors walk and the operator follows them, the shot jumps all over the place until the camera settles on another good frame. That tiny readjustment after you've settled isn't too good either. With "walk and talks," the camera operator needs to find and coordinate with the rhythm of the actors. You don't want to be going up in movement as the actors are going down.

CRANES / JIBS:

A crane is a wonderful tool to have on set. The camera is placed on the end of a long crane arm that has heavy

4.10. A crane in use on set. Photo: Laura Radford.

weights on the back end, allowing the camera arm to be elevated enough to achieve fantastic high-angle or sweeping shots. We have all seen shots starting on the cowboy's face as he rides past camera and off into the sunset; the camera cranes up, and the end credits roll. It can be used in dramatic circumstances like this, or to subtly rise up over a fence to reveal a house for an exterior shot. But just because the camera can move on the crane doesn't mean it has to. You may just be after a really high angle looking down on your actors. Some cranes have a hot-head on the end allowing the operator to control pans or tilts from the floor. Others have seats for the operator and focus puller / director. Some smaller versions, called mini-jibs, don't rise as high and have the camera fixed in the same position.

4.11. A Steadicam operator on set. Photo: Joe Bullen.

STEADICAM / GIMBAL:

The introduction of the Steadicam in 1976 revolutionized film and video. Over the past three decades, the Steadicam has been an invaluable, dynamic production tool. It enables smooth shots as a camera operator follows actors and runs through corridors. It was originally adapted from the military, who had large, heavy machine guns on metallic, movable arms attached to helicopters. It allowed the user to move the gun with ease and not shoulder the weight. So now we have a heavy camera attached to an arm connected to a harness worn by an operator. The Steadicam also allows you to do camera moves a dolly cannot. Using a Steadicam is also quite expensive, but can save time if you can't lay track or don't want the look of handheld.

A gimbal is like a Steadicam: it captures smooth images and reduces jerkiness by stabilizing the camera. The Steadicam is more expensive and is superior, but gimbals are smaller, less cumbersome, and can work in places the Steadicam can't and with a smaller price tag. They can also be used with a second operator manipulating the pan and tilt of the camera with a remote-control unit, independent of the gimbal's movement.

4.12. A camera and gimbal on set.

AERIAL / DRONES:

Aerial photography used to be limited to helicopters with special camera mounts, but now drones have conquered the market. A drone is a small, radio-controlled flying unit that can carry a camera underneath it to capture wonderful aerial footage once only available from a helicopter. They can reach heights of several thousand feet, although most countries prohibit them being used above a certain altitude. (In the U.K., for example, permission must be gained from the CAA (Civil Aviation Authority) to fly a unit higher than 400 feet.) Drones normally require two people to control it: one pilot and one camera operator. Drone operators must be well

qualified, have their own insurance, and be approved by the CAA in the United Kingdom and the FAA (Federal Aviation Administration) in the United States. There are also restrictions when using drones flying near the general public or over private land.

CONNOTATION — WHAT DOES IT MEAN?

What are the connotations of a shot? Connotation means "associated meaning." The opposite of this, denotation, means "literal meaning." The connotations of the color "red" are danger, warning, passion, blood . . . It's important to consider the connotations

4.13. A drone in action. Photo: Uppercut Productions.

of lighting when shooting something. It's your instinct, really telling you what it means to both you and the audience. Thinking about what your shot might mean helps you in your decision-making process and your approach in how to capture it. An unbalanced frame can break your ideal composition to show that a character is a little shifty. Or in order to make a character appear a little warmer, I might not use a color temperature blue (CTB) gel to correct a tungsten light during a daylight scene. Maybe there's a character sitting in a bar who's so stressed and fed up with life, they're about to have an emotional breakdown. You could frame that bright red, out-of-focus, flashing neon light behind the bar next to his head. You're subtly using color and framing to reflect their thoughts. Cinematography is all about

feeling and emotion; how can you use your skills to convey these feelings and emotions on screen?

A great example demonstrating ingenious framing comes from the British film *Wondrous Oblivion* (2003). The film tells the story of David, an 11-year-old boy in the 1960s who loves playing cricket but isn't particularly good at it. A Jamaican family moves in next door, and the father (Delroy Lindo) builds a cricket net in the back garden. One scene sees David's mother dealing with a leaking tap. The father from next door comes in to help. They slowly get closer and closer and wetter and wetter trying to mop the floor together. Something intimate is happening between them, and the camera's positioning is ingenious. It is placed under the kitchen table with one of the table legs squarely center

4.14. The camera is hiding in this shot from *Wondrous Oblivion* (2003).

frame. Since this could have easily been moved by production, why is it there? *It offers the connotation of spying.* We shouldn't be watching this, as either it shouldn't be happening or is a very private moment. If the camera were a person hiding, moving to see behind the table leg would risk detection by the people in the scene. As David comes home from school and interrupts the action, the camera rises up from underneath the table. Everything is once again traditionally framed since the moment between the mother and the neighbor has been broken.

THREE-POINT LIGHTING

How do we light, and where do we start? These questions puzzled me

as a younger filmmaker. The options and possibilities seemed unlimited. However, once you start approaching each scene with a certain under-standing and knowledge, everything becomes a little clearer. Maybe you're a director who needs to know a little more about lighting, or a camera operator looking to get more insight. Let's recap lighting fundamentals.

My first introduction to lighting was bouncing a redhead light (800W tung-sten) with a full CTB gel onto a white ceiling above the set. The bounced light created a soft ambient glow that raised the exposure in the room, already a little dark, and the gel converted the color temperature from tungsten to daylight (to match the daylight coming in from a doorway). Then I started to learn about augmenting.

Look around your location. Where is the light coming from? Is it hard or soft light? What color is it? Are there multiple sources? Take your cues regarding the intensity and color of the light from this analysis, and begin from there. Most lighting is either supporting or adding to what's already present on location. Starting from scratch on a set or studio means you're going to be emulating the natural environment.

Start with motivated light or a "supposed" motivated light source already established. It could be a window or a practical light, or something the audience could justify as a light source. A practical light is any light that is part of the scene. It could be an overhead light bulb, desk lamp, torch, or firelight, and these are great motivational sources to work from. Sometimes, that source is enough to light your actors for you, but you can also use it as a guide or starting point to be augmented by film lights. Practicals such as desk lamps might need a dimmer to be attached to reduce their intensity, or could even be fitted with a smaller-watt bulb. This way the light plays within the scene without overexposing your image. Use these as your motivation to light your scene. Maybe the practical light by the bedside is too dim for the scene and too hard on your actor's face, but a 1K tungsten lamp with a soft box around it, just out of

shot, might give you a more pleasing and realistic feel. The audience, of course, sees the bedside lamp and thinks the light on the actor is all from that single source.

Three-point lighting goes back to the 1930s, when Hollywood actors were all lit a certain way. I like to think of it as a foundation, a starting point from which you can move on and tweak. The three main lights in three-point lighting are:

KEY LIGHT:

The main light source in the scene. This can be light from the window, a desk lamp, or (if you're outside) the sun. It can be artificial light or natural light. A good starting position for the key light is at a 45-degree angle between your talent and the camera, and at a 45-degree downward angle. This is commonly known as the "45 / 45 rule." ("Rule" of course meaning a good starting point.) You set the exposure on the camera by this key light.

BACKLIGHT:

Backlight, as its name suggests, backlights the actors. Placed behind them, the light creates a rim or halo light around their back, head, or shoulders to bring them out from the background. Picture a person wearing a black suit in a darkroom. A backlight would define them and show us their form against the darkness.

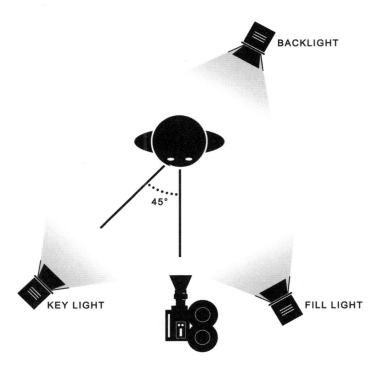

4.15. Three-point lighting in action.

FILL LIGHT:

Fill light "fills" in the shadows caused by the key light. It's normally placed on the opposite side of the camera to the key light, and is of a lesser intensity in order for us to see the effects of the key light. If the fill light was the same intensity, you wouldn't see any shadows at all since the two lights would balance each other out. You set the mood of the shot using this fill light.

Look at this example on the next page from *Wonder Woman* (2017) (Gal Gadot) to see three-point lighting in action. Keyed from the right-hand side of the frame, there is a little fill on the left and very strong backlight.

Three-point lighting demonstrates positions, but the "lights" might not all be actual film lights. Lighting and cinematography aren't necessarily about big lighting units and everything on a big scale. They're also about choosing the right tools for the job. Let's imagine we have an actor in a room for one shot and we need to light them. Perhaps there is already lovely, soft sunlight coming through the window. We would take advantage of that perfect timing. It's only one shot,

4.16. Wonder Woman (Gal Gadot) lit, demonstrating three-point lighting.

so we don't need to keep that light source steady. For our fill light we'd use a white reflector, or maybe a piece of poly-board to bounce the sunlight onto the other side of the actor's face. Finally, there is a tiny desk lamp or hallway light on behind them providing backlight. We've achieved three-point lighting using no artificial light sources. You might decide to leave the reflector out of it and let the fill side of their face go darker, and maybe even scratch the backlight to make the shot still darker and moodier. You designed the shot with the three-point lighting in mind, and either decided to use all three or just the ones you wanted. It was a good foundation and a good starting point.

When lighting, put the camera in place first. You need to see the image you're getting through the lens. Ask the actor to run the action. When you start positioning lights, if there

are any practical lights playing in the scene — overhead strip lights, desk lamps, torches — turn them on so that you can see what you're working with within the scene. Then light from the back of the set first and work your way to the actor and their practical light. Make sure you turn off any house or studio working light; these will interfere with your setup.

What if you're in a dark corridor or tunnel? The only light sources are single bare bulbs on the ceiling, or battery-operated or naked flame torches. The actor's torch or the bulbs then becomes the key light. If an actor's face is not easily read, perhaps bring in a fill light to lift the exposure. This could be a reflector for bounce, or even a diffused tungsten light bouncing into some poly-board. Then you're using bounce to fill their faces, giving the impression the torch light is causing that. Ensure any additional lights you bring in match the color temperature of the light sources already in the shot. If you were augmenting fire, this would be a tungsten light with some full color temperature orange (CTO) around it to bring the temperature of the tungsten source (3200K) down to match the fire at 1800K.

Set and position your key light so that you can see highlights in each actor's eyes. A highlight in one of the eyes looks good, but a highlight in both is even better. They say the eyes are the windows to the soul, and they are an actor's main tool to convey emotion. An "eye light" is a light shone directly onto an actor's eyes to bring them out more and make their eyes "pop" on camera.

When blocking your action and setting up the shot, keep the camera on the darker fill side of the actor's face. The key light illuminates the actor, wrapping around their face

and gradually getting darker towards the camera. Watching the texture be revealed on an actor or object is very pleasing. If you shoot on the same side as the key, it might look a little flat since the exposure is even across the subject's face. Take a look at the example below where we see Daniel Craig as James Bond in *Spectre* (2015). See how the light is brighter on the other side of the face where the key light is? Had Craig looked to the other side of the camera, the camera would then immediately be on the key side, not the fill side, and this approach wouldn't have the desired effect. Notice the highlights in both eyes too.

Extra steps are needed when lighting and filming older actors. You want to make them look the best they can. Highlighting all their skin imperfections, lines, and blemishes wouldn't make you a very popular DP. When lighting older subjects, bring

4.17. Shooting on the fill side of Daniel Craig as James Bond in *Spectre* (2015).

the key light around to the front a little more than usual, almost next to the camera. This key light would now be almost all fill light, causing no shadows at all. This light fills in all the marks and contours of the face, making the older subject look better. We start with the three-point lighting model, adjusting it to suit the film or our subject's needs. You need to allow for this in the blocking phase to ensure our approach works. Look at this example from the James Bond film *Casino Royale* (2006). The scene is blocked so Bond (Daniel Craig) is shot on the fill side of the light coming from the table lamp, and M (Judi Dench) is positioned more front on so the light fills her face.

4.18. This scene is staged to allow M (Judi Dench) to be lit more from the front, reducing shadows.

SHOOTING ON THE FILL SIDE IN BOTH DIRECTIONS

If the motivated light source is well established on a particular side of your actors, blocking the scene out to shoot on the fill side shouldn't be a problem. However, the blocking might mean two actors face the same direction while sitting and talking at a bus shelter or in a hospital waiting room. So can we maintain shooting on the fill side for both reverse angles when we film each of their single shots? Yes, if you're very crafty. Once you've established the key light from one side, subtly reverse it to the opposite side of the other actor to uniformly maintain your aesthetic. This only works in an environment with fairly soft, evenly spread ambient light devoid of strong, identifiable light sources. The ratio between the key light and fill light must be very low. Maybe it's a bright pub or bar, a school, or an office location. With light all around, the audience won't notice that the light on the opposite side of each angle is in fact a little brighter. Look at the example on the next page from *Wonder Woman* (2017) of two cross-cutting reverse angles to see how the key light jumps from one side to the other, allowing us to keep the aesthetic and maintain shooting on the fill side.

4.19. Shooting on the fill side in both directions as seen in *Wonder Woman* (2017).

SHOOTING DAY EXTERIORS

When shooting outside during the day, your main key light is the sun. The sun is a hard source of light that creates hard, often unflattering shadows on people's faces. Hard light from the sun can be naturally diffused when it passes behind clouds, creating a softer light. You can't control the sun's position directly, but you can control when you film and how you position your actors, so block your scene accordingly. When shooting daylight exteriors, decide on a mood and commit, maintaining this atmosphere throughout the sequence. Cloudy and overcast, or hot and sunny. The decision might be made for you on the day, but if the sun is in and out of the clouds, you have to be able to work with the weather. Using the sun as a backlight provides a lovely halo around your actors; you might then fill in their faces by using poly-board

or a reflector to bounce light from the sun. Another alternative would be to use an HMI light on location, power permitting. Some cinematographers like to position their actors so they're always backlit. They plan the shooting day and ensure each actor is filmed with their back is to the sun. This might be cheating, but it sure does look good. In theory, were the sun directly overhead, both actors might have light falling on them from behind. If you know the sun will backlight the scene well at 4 pm, don't schedule a 9 am shoot. It's all about working with the environment to create the best-looking shots possible.

Take a look at these two matching shots from the end of *L.A. Confidential* (1997) where both the actors are backlit by the sun. This shouldn't work — there aren't two suns — but we accept it as both shots look similar and match. It's bright and high key for the end of the movie, and is a nice

4.20. Both actors backlit by the sun in *L.A. Confidential* (1997).

example of what you can get away with if the audience is immersed in the story and characters.

Butterfly diffusion frames are superb tools for outside shooting. Large 6' × 6', 8' × 8', 12' × 12', and 20' × 20' frames hold diffusion material of varying strengths and thicknesses such as silk, grid cloth, or muslin to turn the harsh sunlight into a more flattering soft light. You still keep the direction of the light, but it's softer and wraps more attractively around your actors' faces. Check out the pictures below to see a diffusion frame on set, and then the before-and-after to see how diffusion softens the light on the actor's face.

Sometimes shooting exteriors may require you to stop down your aperture to f/8, f/11, or even more, affecting your depth of field. It's common practice in these conditions to use ND filters to cut the light down instead, either in the camera itself or as separate filters in the matte box. This would enable you to open to a wider aperture of f/4 or f/2.8.

WITHOUT DIFFUSION   WITH DIFFUSION

4.21. A butterfly frame with diffusion softening the light on an actor.

When shooting daylight exteriors throughout a full day, adjust your color temperature to follow the natural color of the light as the day progresses. The color temperature might go from 4900K to 5600K, and then to 5200K. Adjusting your color temperature slightly as you go maintains the light's color consistency.

Look at lighting breakdown 4.22 (color insert) to see a butterfly frame with diffusion in action, softening the hard sunlight on the actor. The scene was staged to keep the camera on the fill side of the actors, allowing the soft sun source to wrap around the face nicely.

NEGATIVE FILL

If fill light fills in the shadow areas by adding light to the darker side of a face, either by reflecting light or using a lamp, what might "negative fill" be? Negative fill subtracts light from areas you might not want it. Fill light uses a whiteboard or reflector to add light, and negative fill uses black cloth or a butterfly frame containing a black solid to reduce light. When shooting outside, light spills everywhere by reflecting and bouncing off objects, walls, and the ground, and negative fill reduces that light spill. Remember how the key light wraps around the face, and its position creates textures of light and dark? Sometimes being outside or in a well-lit room means light spills everywhere, so you can't clearly define the key light's position — too much natural fill has compromised the actor's texture. Taking light away enhances the key light, sculpting, and facial definition. If you are filming an exterior wide shot, these frames of negative fill could be as large as 20' × 20' to block the sun and control the light.

SHOOTING DAY INTERIORS

Shooting day or even night interiors, you'll find yourself either on location in real environments or in a studio

4.23. A black solid removing light from the actor to create more texture on their face.

setting. In both instances, the principles and motivations around your light sources will be the same.

With daylight interiors, the light sources will most likely be the windows. Unless the script specifies what the time of day is, you can shoot whenever best serves your light angle and color. Depending on budget, you might use outside lights firing in through the windows, maybe a 2.5K HMI or 6K, 12K, or even an 18K. There could be diffusion in front of these, depending on how soft you want it to be. If windows do appear in shot and seem a little hot (brighter), it's fine because we know it's often a little brighter outside than inside. Once your illumination comes in, consider adding a little fill light to raise the exposure. If you're not lighting from the outside, you'll only be augmenting what is already coming in naturally through the window. You can have lights set up inside, duplicating the color temperature and softness to match the natural daylight in play. When shooting in a studio, I set up soft light coming through the window, but also have a tiny streak of hard light (which could even be a little overexposed) firing onto a small area of the set. The actors may or may not walk through it, but this tiny addition can sell the realness of your environment. It's almost like you couldn't quite control that overexposed "real" daylight.

On location, your scene might require you to mix interiors and exteriors, filming action both inside and outside (through a window) simultaneously. Perhaps your scene involves someone inside looking out the window, anticipating someone else about to approach the garden path. For the camera to see the person on the path and expose properly, the aperture would be stopped down to f/11 or so. The inside, however, is now very dark, so you have two options. You could bring in lights to up the exposure of the room and better match the exterior, or you could place sheets of neutral density (ND) gel over the windows. If outside is f/11 and inside (without using lights) is f/4, you will require an ND gel of 0.9 strength, which is the equivalent of three stops on your aperture.

Shooting daylight interiors might sometimes mean simply softening the sunlight outside and using a few reflectors as fill. For speed and ease of shooting, you could block and position your actors accordingly to exploit the natural window light already in play.

Look at lighting breakdown 4.24 (color insert) to see one way to light a day interior. We have a 2.5K HMI behind diffusion as our key light through the window, a Kino Flo backlighting the actor sitting down, and finally some smoke for extra atmosphere. No fill light required.

SHOOTING NIGHT EXTERIORS

Night shoots demand much consideration. Firstly, you'll feel it in your budget. Shooting at night requires more light (and possibly power generators), more food and drink (to energize the cast and crew), and usually more time, too. People work slightly slower, and reduced visibility compromises safety. Almost everything takes longer when shooting at night. Also, for single one-off shots needing a "night" look, consider shooting in twilight. There is still some detail in the evening clouds, and a little more light for you then too. You then have the option of grading the image darker in post to suit your creative needs. There's also "day-for-night" shooting. You can get creative with your camera; turn your color temperature to tungsten or even lower to make the sky and image look a little cooler and bluer. Then, stop down your aperture and darken the image a little. Make sure you film in soft light conditions so there are no hard shadows from the sun. If it's a tiny scene or a one-off shot, this method might save time and money.

If the scene has to be shot at night, consider generators for power, although they have to be positioned quite a distance away to avoid causing issues for the sound department. New portable, battery-powered LED light panels are a consideration for smaller, intimate scenes, and nullify the need to rent a generator. With night exteriors with no identifiable source of light (like streetlights), you have to get creative. Filming in woods or in open fields always poses a few issues. What you are then striving for is the "illusion" of night. Once the audience has bought it, you might get away with quite a bit. When filming night exteriors, first backlight the scene. This could be your moon in an open space or wooded environment, or street lights if shooting in a suburban setting. How colorful should your moonlight be? Some go full blue; others might use a little blue with an added hint of green. That decision is up to you. If you're lighting your actors' faces add a little fill light to match the moon or backlight. Night exterior lighting is also generally a harder light since it comes from a specific source, not general ambient fill.

Look at lighting breakdown 4.25 (color insert) to see an example of lighting a night exterior. We have a 2.5K HMI as a hard 3 / 4 backlight (also the key light in this example) and a 2.5K HMI through diffusion as fill from the front. Both are gelled with ½ CTB (color temperature blue) to give a cool moonlight feel, and some smoke is added for a bit of atmosphere.

SHOOTING NIGHT INTERIORS

Night interiors generally involve the use of a harder light. What sources do you have in the scene or are you trying to create? There could be practical lights, overhead lights or desk lamps, a torch, candles, fire, or even moonlight or street light spilling through windows. Most scenes will play better if you can show the light source. Sometimes you can take your motivational cues from those practical lights and use them imaginatively in your setups. Then it's about augmenting those practical lights with the lights you have on set. You might find that the practical is powerful enough to light your scene, or perhaps it could be helped by your film lights. Don't be afraid to have your actors dip or walk into dark areas either. We, as the audience, are aware of the environment, and it is perfectly acceptable to have your talent go dark momentarily. When shooting night interiors, only using a key light and backlight (and not using much fill light) might identify the sources a little more.

Look at lighting breakdown 4.26 (color insert) to see an example of lighting a night interior. We have a 2.5K HMI gelled with a ½ CTB firing in from outside to suggest moonlight and act as the primary source of light. There is also a 1 x 1 LED panel dialed to 5600K inside the room, also gelled with ½ CTB to match the HMI outside. The LED acts as an extension of the HMI to help the light wrap around the actor's face more towards camera.

This approach is aiming for that single source look with no fill light.

This next lighting breakdown would also be considered a night interior, but the cues for motivated light sources are a little more inventive since the film is set inside a space capsule. This sequence was shot on a studio set, not on location. The director and production designer added practical lights to the scene: two fluorescent tubes down the back of the set connected to a dimmer board. These played nicely on camera, matching the environment and providing a motivating source for the majority of light in the capsule. A soft top light was provided by a 2K blonde firing through muslin. A 650W Fresnel gelled with ½ CTS (color temperature straw) was placed outside the window for a motivating sun source. Finally, a LED unit providing a soft light source was placed to the side to give some texture to the actor's face. This was an extension of light from above and spill from the center window. Look at lighting breakdown 4.27 (color insert) to see it in action.

USING SMOKE

Smoke can be a wonderful tool in the cinematographer's arsenal. Smoke produced by a smoke machine doesn't resemble smoke from a fire on camera. The device is used instead to create atmosphere. Having smoke in your shot also diffuses light and highlights the light source. If you have a light source outside of a window beaming into the set, pumping smoke into the room will create a wonderful shaft of light and make your visuals more dynamic. To use smoke on set, close the doors and windows, fill the room with smoke, and let it settle for a few minutes. What you're after is for the smoke to be present, but not still whirling around the room, an obvious distraction to the audience. If you were filming in a dusty attic or basement and wanted to create the sense that no one had been there for a while, smoke would do nicely. Or maybe you want to reduce the contrast in the shot to create a nice, soft, cozy environment around a fireplace; smoke would diffuse the light, spreading it into the shadows and helping you achieve this. Smoke will naturally disperse over time, however. You

might have a wonderful, atmospheric wide shot, but by the time you get the closer shots of the actors, the smoke's presence will be lessened. Make sure you keep topping up the smoke levels in the room to maintain continuity.

A haze machine is similar to a smoke machine, but a little more subtle. It still produces the same effect, but it's a little less dense. If you can get your hands on a smoke machine, the effect it produces might make your visuals more interesting. Here's an example from *Lord of the Rings: The Fellowship of the Ring* (2001).

CHEATING WITH LIGHT

Sometimes you'll need to be very creative with your light sources and their motivations. Lighting usually needs to be motivated from a source with a justified position. Having your

4.28. Smoke on set producing a shaft of light in *Lord of the Rings: The Fellowship of the Ring* (2001).

actors run through a field at night means some sort of moonlight will likely hang overhead and light the scene. As with any creative endeavor, you are allowed a degree of artistic license. How much license you take is up to you and how much you can get away with. When it comes to reality and the audience's beliefs, there is room for creative boundary-pushing. *Good images trump absolute realism and matching. Audiences don't care about 100% realism as long as they're engrossed by the film, so feel free to push these boundaries.* Audiences won't say, "The lighting didn't look very good, but at least it was 100% representative of the environment"; they'll just come away feeling a little unimpressed with the quality of the film and not really knowing why. I'm not saying have a red light for the moon or have your cast completely lit up like a Christmas tree. But if that moonlight is coming from above and behind them, and might not stretch around to light their faces and eyes as you'd like, you should light your cast the way you want to. Make them look better than what the *realistic* way might suggest. So if you need to cheat how far a light from a window creeps onto an actor's face so that you can make the star look better, do it.

Lighting mismatches are also creative obstacles, but you can push the boundaries to suit your needs and the needs of the film. Look at

the example below. Here we see two stills from the film *The Last Samurai* (2003) featuring Tom Cruise and Ken Watanabe. On the first shot of Watanabe, a lovely backlight separates him from the night sky. Then in the reverse shot, over his shoulder on the other actor, we see a hint of that light, but its intensity is so diminished from the previous shot that the two don't match at all. This isn't an error on the part of DP John Toll, though. If they had kept it the same, we'd see a large bright blue area of the frame, distracting us from the emotional moment between a father and his dying son.

4.29. Cheating with light, as seen in *The Last Samurai* (2003).

Adhering to the lighting sources, their intensity, and their positions 100% of the time might be stopping you from creating some really interesting images. Don't get tied in knots sticking to what is absolutely right and correct for the environment you're in and lose the opportunity to create images that not only look good, but also fit the story. You can have both and bend the rules a little, and the audience will never know.

LIGHTING THE STAR

In the golden age of Hollywood, some stars would only be lit by a particular director of photography and said as much in their contracts. They had to be lit a certain way, and sometimes only on one side of their face. The studios were very protective of their stars, and no matter what the character endured — a hurricane, fire, or any kind of trauma — they always managed to keep their stunning looks. In today's movies, things are a little more realistic, but only just. Actors still need to look good; they're what the audience has paid to see. As a director of photography, you must be aware of how particular actors look in different types of light, hard and soft, and if they have a "good side" from which they like to be photographed. This can be established by filming lighting tests of your actors before the actual shoot. Actors of a certain age might have skin imperfections, lines, or blemishes. Masking these might require a little more fill light or the use of diffusion in front of the camera. Perhaps your hero takes his

shirt off, so you move the key light a little farther to the side of him to accentuate his muscle definition. You could also drop the camera a little lower than normal to give him a more imposing or confident look. A scene's realism is only one element to consider when lighting your cast.

When filming actors, soft light is generally better. That's not to say you shouldn't use hard light; sometimes it's warranted. But you can still create that sense of mood *and* have your actors look good by using softer light. Soft light can come in various strengths depending on setup. Or maybe you're filming the older villain of the film, mean and hard, so you use hard light with a bit of diffusion to take the edge off slightly. Experiment and see what works best.

Light sets and people from the back of the shot to the front. Light the background and work back toward the camera and actors. If you light the actor first, and the director says, "Great. Let's shoot!" you then must concede that the background hasn't yet been lit. Then it's a waiting game: the clock is ticking and you feel pressured because the director thought you were ready when you were not. Lighting back to front means that you've done your job so that when the director says, "Great. Let's shoot!" you say, "Sure!" It's just good practice.

CHAPTER 5

DIRECTING YOUR BLOCKBUSTER

"The job of a film director is to tell the story through the juxtaposition of uninflected images."
— DAVID MAMET, SCREENWRITER / DIRECTOR

Directing involves good casting, setting the tone and style of the film, working with the actors on set, and using the camera to tell a story, all while bringing your "vision" to the screen. As a director you need a strong vision and a broad overview of the entire film. The entire project should be in your head in one shape or form so you can consistently maintain tone, pace, and feel. Directing is also the ability to think in cuts. How do you see the scenes edited together? Directors use their intuition and understanding of human emotion to augment their craft and technical abilities. Directing blockbusters is hard, stressful work, but also a lot of fun. The director works primarily with the director of photography, production designer, and costume supervisor to nail down the look of the film. Each department has to be on the same page, and it's the director's responsibility to make sure this happens.

SHOT LISTS, STORYBOARDS, AND SHOOTING TIMES

Here's the first tip when writing out your shot list: keep them short. A one-line description is enough to jog your memory what is up next: "Wide — whole scene, dolly," "CU Dan, whole scene, 50 mm?" These short, tight descriptions mean I can see what I'm shooting next at a glance, which helps

85

me work fast. For basic shot lists, be concise and brief. You need to be able to get the information quickly, not lines and lines of superfluous text. You then shoot, crossing off the shots as you go.

I like to storyboard anything involving stunts, special effects, or visual effects. It's important to convey to other departments what each shot requires. If it's just characters talking in a room, I don't need to have that drawn out; I can readily find those shots on set, a process I enjoy. Communicate your wants clearly and quickly to your grips, stunt team, and special effects technician. They might be able to suggest a better angle to capture the stunt or effect, or just confirm they know their responsibilities. There is a danger of storyboarding everything and becoming too attached to the images you've been agonizing over for weeks. After I've suggested an alternative shooting angle, directors have told me that it "has to be exactly this." There is a tendency to force you into a fixed idea of how the shots have to be. Unyieldingly adhering to the story-boards may cause you to miss much better options right in front of you.

A good rule of thumb when preparing your shot list and schedule is to think of each shot taking between 20–25 minutes to shoot. That includes setting up the camera, blocking, lighting, rehearsing, and shooting. So

a 12-hour shooting day (with an hour for lunch) gives you between 25 and 33 shots daily. If you have two hours of the shooting day left and seven shots on the list to go, that could be quite a push. Many shots take longer to execute than 20 minutes; some may take just five. But they balance out. And of course I mean doing things properly: rehearsing, and filming using lights and flags to sculpt the light. Give yourself fewer shots on the first day of your shoot — aim for 15, not 25. The crew always needs time to set up and find their feet. Setting an unreasonable goal for day one and failing may reverberate and shape the remainder of the project.

TONE AND STYLE — WHAT LOOK AND FEEL ARE YOU GOING FOR?

Perhaps one of the most important parts of directing is tone. Once you know the tone of your film, you can make smart, relevant decisions about everything that follows. Tone is some-thing that will come to you as you read the script: the pace, the feel, the style. Tone must be set very early on screen and in a stylistic way. If you know the tone, you know how fast to move the dolly or how dark that scene should be. You can better make deci-sions on camera style, performance, and the set, or colors for grading come post-production. Knowing tone early on grounds all your subsequent creative choices. Tone tells me about my opening shot, the background music, and the like. It sets the pace and lets the audience know what they're watching.

Style is very subjective, isn't it? Each director does it differently. Action director Michael Bay likes to fill his frames with sun flares, fast dolly moves, and saturated colors. Clint Eastwood likes to take his time, gracefully moving his actors through the frame and having the characters tell him when to cut. Paul Greengrass likes to shoot in a documentary style, finding the frame (and the focus!) as he goes. Jean-Pierre Jeunet likes to use very wide-angle lenses close to his actors.

Style comes out of what you like, your sensibilities, and what the story requires. Style also dictates your coverage. If you want fast and frantic cuts like director Edgar Wright (*Hot Fuzz*, *Baby Driver*), then you are going to need lots of shots to make up these sequences. You can't just say to the editor, "Make it fast like Edgar Wright" without having the material.

How you decide to film your script is up to you and your DP. The way you frame your shots, your characters, and their surroundings matters greatly. Are you planning smooth, graceful camera moves on a dolly, or are you on a tripod? Are you letting the characters play out the story, and your camera merely covers the action? Maybe you feel the script calls for everything to

be handheld and on the shoulder to give it a sense of immediacy? Maybe you're going for a documentary-style approach, the frame comprised of zooms in and out and similar gonzo camerawork. What is important is that you don't arbitrarily apply a style to your film without it serving the story. Don't decide to shoot your new film handheld and have constant whip pans because a film you just saw used that approach. And not everything has to be "dark and gritty." Some very good films have aesthetics that are high-key, flat, and fairly static. These decisions must come from a creative and narrative place. You're doing your project a disservice by emulating films whose pace or style differ vastly from yours. *Your script is its own beast, and demands its own distinctive style based on the story's characters and events.* On previous projects, I've shot scenes where everything up to the time the character left town or quit his job was on the tripod. Then, once the story kicked into gear, it was all handheld. But if you're shooting out of order, knowing which bits you're shooting in the story and when helps ensure your styles match. Read the script while shooting at least once a week. This way you are reminded of the story as a whole, and where you are in it.

I've worked on projects when the director has said they don't mind if we lose focus momentarily or we're finding things a little with the frame.

I'm happy to go with that loose, more documentary approach, but beware of a style that is talked about but, just by circumstance, never really materialises. It turned out our focus puller was very talented and we never lost focus until one shot on the last day. When asked if we should go again, the director replied, "No. It was all part of the style as discussed." However, although discussed, it never was actually implemented, and to now let that one singular shot through risks the appearance of poor photography. Likewise, an editing style has to be established by using it repeatedly before we can then give over finding focus shots or fast flashy cuts to that label. If you fail to establish it, you might look technically inefficient — so beware.

Listen to your intuition, as it's constantly telling you how things should be filmed or performed. Try to mix both the instinctual and technical feel of a scene. Approaching the shots or scenes through characters' feelings and emotions may reveal your ideal shooting strategy.

MAKING THINGS CINEMATIC —
COMPOSITION, COVERAGE, DEVELOPING SHOTS, DEPTH, AND VISUAL STORYTELLING

Telling your story in a more cinematic way does many things for your film. It helps the audience accept and give themselves over to the world you've created; it keeps them involved emotionally; and it helps set up and sell your gorgeous set or location. *It also gives your blockbuster heaps of production value and an epic feel.* For this to work well, you must have a good understanding of cinematography and editing; the two go hand in hand. Let's break each aspect down, because you'll have a much better, sophisticated movie if you can implement these ideas.

This section is perhaps one of the most important for cinematographers and directors. I learned these lessons the hard way. After a shoot, I used to have a niggling notion that the footage or film that I had produced didn't match what it felt like on location, or wasn't as good as what I had hoped. It didn't look like the movies I was used to seeing at the theater! Why was that? It very rarely had anything to do with budget. Sometimes you can't afford the dolly or crane or hundreds of extras, but you could have the exact same location and tools as the next crew, who make a blockbuster fit for the big screen while your movie looks like a soap or student film. The difference is *how* they shoot it.

Let's start with something small and easily achievable.

COMPOSITION:
Whatever shot you have planned to film your action, frame a little wider.

Wider shots allow the audience to see more of a location, more set, and offer a better idea of place and feel. Close-ups become medium close-ups. Medium close-ups become medium shots . . . Composing a wider shot means part of the environment creeps into the frame and helps anchor the character to their surrounding more too. Reassess your camera's height. Does dropping lower allow you to capture the striking stained-glass windows in the church, selling the gorgeous location your characters find themselves in? These small tweaks to the frame can make all the difference.

COVERAGE:

Coverage refers to all the different shots needed to get the whole of a scene filmed. Good coverage is part of the staging and blocking phase, and it's best to stage a scene to have as few cuts as possible. This approach forces you to stage in depth (coming up shortly) and move the actors or camera to accommodate this idea, thus making the action more interesting.

Let's start at the beginning. If we had two characters in a scene, the more traditional method is Master, Single, Single or Wide, Shot / Reverse Shot. A wide of the action, then two separate single angles on each character. This approach has long served all of Hollywood and its use is widespread. This is just how the scene is

shot; there are many ways it might be edited together. We would have a wide or master shot of the action, and then two single shots — mediums, medium close-ups, or close-ups of each actor also of the entire scene. Even though the wide was shot first, the editor might start the scene on the close-up of one character, then show a close-up of the other before revealing the wide shot. It can play 50 / 50 on each character as they say their lines, or 80% on one character, the other character talking off-camera for the majority of the scene. Obviously things grow a little bigger if we have more active people in the scene. Master, Single, Single is a good, solid starting point — the whole scene is "covered" and in the can. This approach is effective if not always outstanding visually. Sometimes the best approach is the simplest one, and the best place for the camera is eye level with no elaborate camera moves. The characters and their emotions come first and should always be front and center.

When planning coverage, a good director or cinematographer is thinking two or three shots ahead rather than just focusing on the shot at hand. If you have a wide shot and two singles to shoot, when blocking roughly see how the singles will photograph and what else might be required. You might have a wide shot, and the first single of Actor A looks good with the window or picture frame in the background, but Actor B might have nothing of interest behind them or be positioned away from a strong light source. A slight adjustment in positioning for the wide shot will enable you to have a more dynamic framing for Actor B, with depth, a doorway, or some other detail now also in the frame. You haven't boxed yourself into a corner or been forced to shoot a poorly considered frame.

I cannot overemphasize the need to *know where your edit points might be.* Have some idea of how you are going to cut from shot to shot, or scene to scene. *Directors must be able to visualize the scene at hand and know how to execute it.* Shooting involves ambiguity, but procuring coverage and doubling up on actions or movements yields contingency options in the edit. See the sequence play out in your head at least one way succinctly; don't just collect footage in hopes the editor can somehow later piece it together. This is why having a background in editing is helpful. Know beforehand how you want to play the scene in the cut, but be prepared to throw that all away if a better suggestion comes your way later. *Always be asking, "How will this shot cut?"*

I find coverage to be a nice safety net. If you've ever found yourself in a situation where your location has changed at the last minute, or a curveball of some kind has presented

itself, or you're just not that prepared, filming traditional Master, Single, Single coverage will ensure you have a viewable scene come the edit. It's a foundation, something you can fall back on should your wonderfully complicated camera staging be ditched for whatever reason. With traditional coverage, you can still use your shots the way you intended, but if a better idea comes late in the edit, you can use the additional shots to assemble the scene differently. Shooting coverage also means you can cut down a scene if your film is running a little long, either for your own sensibilities or to fit a broadcast transmission or festival. If your scenes are all single developing shots, you are stuck with them; however beautiful they may be, their length can't change. Know when to use lots of coverage and when to focus on developing shots.

When shooting, overlap the sequence from various angles, giving your editor flexibility with when and how to cut the sequence together. You never want to be in the edit saying, "We have to use that shot — it's the only one we have of the woman walking up to the house," or whatever the problem might be. If you have the option on set for the actor to move to their position or start in frame, have them move first.

Once you've shot your coverage and the scene is over, mentally put your shots together. Run through the shots you've filmed with the DP and cast. Was everything covered? Objects, looks, glances, inserts? Then anything missing will present itself. You don't want to realize you missed shots when you're sitting in your edit suite.

Be mindful if an actor says something about saving his or her performance for the close-up or single shots. This is common and makes sense from their point of view, as you'd likely be in close for the meat of the scene. However, what happens if you get to the edit and decide to play the scene on the wide or the two shot? Then the performance (and the scene) are half of what they could be. Your performers must produce, even on the wider angles.

You might decide to cover the scene in just one shot and film it forgoing the single angles. Keeping it simple might entail filming from just one angle, but still keeping things visually interesting and maintaining that cinematic quality. Director Robert Zemeckis had a scene in his thriller, *What Lies Beneath* (2000), where Harrison Ford and Michelle Pfeiffer were talking in a car crossing a bridge. He could have covered the scene with a two shot from the front of the car and cross-shot two singles through the side windows. All perfectly acceptable. What Zemeckis did, though, was film from behind the actors in one single shot and show the characters only in the car's available mirrors. A very inventive and cinematic way of telling the story and covering the action.

THE DEVELOPING SHOT:
By taking a little care blocking and staging a scene, either by moving the camera or the characters in a shot,

5.1. Covering the action in one shot, as seen in *What Lies Beneath* (2000).

the frame is kept busy for a longer period. This way you don't need to cut; the editing is done in camera by having the characters move into a different shot size or having the camera pull back or push in on them as the scene plays out. Shots that evolve this way are called "developing shots," and are better used for dialogue sequences than action. Action necessitates more cuts to help the pace and get more information across quickly. Gradually revealing information over the course of a shot keeps it alive. Don't give all that information to the audience straight away. Start closer on the action, and either pan or pull back on a dolly or crane. You then reveal something: a person listening, a hole in the road ahead, a sign. You could have your wide shot intentionally not show the whole environment, but as the characters move to the other side of the room, to get something or look out the window, the rest of the space gives us new information.

In one continuous shot, we basically capture all our angles. Not cutting suggests a real sense of intimacy with our characters. Editing can sometimes destroy rhythm; staging involves fewer cuts and keeps the audience immersed. Let the scene dictate whether the shot should be covered in a developing master or with lots of separate coverage. A scene involving fast-paced dialogue and cuts to other

characters' reaction shots would not benefit from a developing one-shot master. Some directors also capture the action in one shot as more of a showy gimmick, something to call attention to itself. Showing off your filmmaking prowess should never be your primary concern. Developing shots can be achieved in one, and sometimes it's a long take with a quick insert to an object, like in the Indiana Jones example below.

Director Steven Spielberg is a master of staging. Look at the scene early in *Raiders of the Lost Ark* (1981) when Marcus Brody (Denholm Elliott) arrives at Indiana Jones (Harrison Ford)'s house. We start on a wide of the door, pan right to see the front room, pan right again to see Indy retrieve a suitcase from the wardrobe, push into a medium single on Marcus, pan left to a wide as we follow Indy to the desk to get his gun, pan right again framing for a two shot as Indy unravels his gun from its cloth, and see an insert of the gun before resuming the wide as Indy throws the gun into his suitcase. This is an efficient method, likely requiring less time to shoot than the seven or eight shots broken down separately. However, you are then stuck with this shot as a whole. You might still lack a needed close-up of a character. The secret to executing shots like this is to block the scene well with your actors and DP. With the shot looking so dynamic and

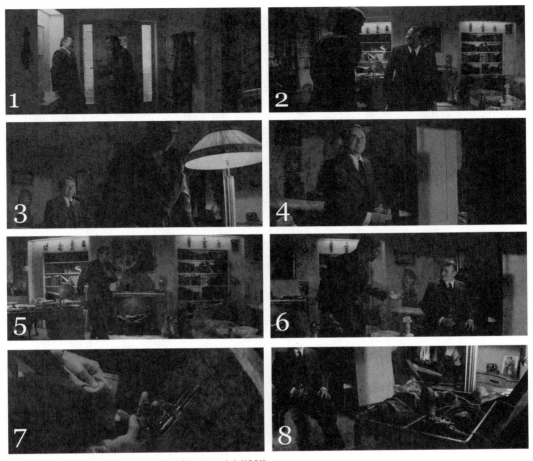

5.2. A developing shot used in *Raiders of the Lost Ark* (1981).

interesting, the audience will hardly notice that you haven't cut.

If you do shoot your scene in a developing shot, it's advisable to have a few cutaways in close-up that are clean and that don't feature any other characters. This device can help cut a scene down or join two takes of the developing shot together. You don't want to feature any over-the-shoulder foreground elements of other characters purely for the reason that you can then cut it in at any point and

not be tied to a particular character's moment or position in the scene. In addition, the camera doesn't have to be continuously moving; it's good to build in small moments of respite where we hold on an angle before we move on. This way the shot can be cut or used in its entirety.

The overall goal is a film with a mixture of nice, cinematic developing shots and more conventionally shot coverage with a Master, Single, Single approach. Go to either extreme and it's all long, uninterrupted developing shots you struggle to cut for length, or endless Master, Single, Single scenes that play pedestrian and boring.

Film director Renny Harlin (*Cliffhanger*, *The Long Kiss Goodnight*) says he likes to achieve one impressive-looking shot a day during production, something that takes a little time to execute and coordinate. Maybe it's a big crane shot, a well-coordinated long take, or an intricate dolly shot. A (roughly) 60-day shooting schedule would mean a visually interesting scene every two or three minutes of the film. Not every shot can be gorgeous, and some will be basic coverage to get information across — but every so often, you can inject something special into your shot list to make a film as visually compelling as can be. So look at your shot list and schedule, whether it's for a feature or a short film, and see where you can work in some kind of visual treat for the audience.

DEPTH:

Once you understand this, you begin to see the angles utilizing the depth every time you compose a shot, and then the standard of your work improves immediately. We've discussed the developing shot approach, and sometimes that necessitates blocking the scene utilizing the depth of the location. Shooting using the depth of any location means finding the long axis of the

environment and placing your camera and action along that axis. So shoot down the corridor, not across it; shoot along the length of the ballroom, not in the corner; position your camera so we see out the doorway and into the other rooms of the house, not just against the flat bedroom wall.

In order to make the scene more dynamic and even to save shooting time, I've often asked myself, "How could we stage this action in one shot?" This forces you to think creatively with your staging, and frame your shots using depth. This might end up being just a single shot, or after blocking and closer inspection you might add a second angle to make the scene work. You're forcing yourself to tell the story without having to cut, compelling you to stage in depth and make the shot more cinematic. Most of the time there is only one camera position that will encapsulate every-thing you need; once found, everything falls into place. How can we frame the crashed car, the cop, his vehicle, and the sunset all in one? Find that angle that lines them all up and shoot. It might mean getting everything in one shot by having the camera really low or really high.

Look at the shot below of Tom Cruise in *Mission: Impossible — Rogue Nation* (2015). After being chased by some bad guys on motor-bikes and crashing his car, Cruise looks up to see them getting away.

5.3. Staging in depth lets you tell your story in fewer shots, seen here in *Mission: Impossible — Rogue Nation* (2015).

Here we see Cruise's shoulder, the bike he's about to jump on to give chase, and the villains escaping on their bikes in the back of the shot. This frame is nicely foreshadowing what is about to happen next.

Try working some element of depth into every shot. Depth helps you tell your story better, orient the audience, and subtly remind viewers where characters are located. Find something on location, or place an object in the foreground frame anchoring the location to each shot. Incorporating the depth of the location might render that extra shot of an object or person superfluous; the audience can already see it in the background or foreground. Here's a shot from *Wonder Woman* (2017) using depth the help orient the audience. We're over Wonder Woman's shoulder as we see reinforcements arriving on the scene of a battle.

5.4. Using depth to help orient the audience, as seen here in *Wonder Woman* (2017).

Depth helps do so many things. Maybe you're shooting a horror or suspense movie; depth could help add tension to the scene. Let's say we have a sequence where some people run into a room while being pursued. They could talk about how they might escape or where they can hide. Maintaining the depth and keeping the entrance doorway in the background keeps the audience on edge — the pursuers might come in at any moment. A framed-off door and a plain wall behind the characters wouldn't have been as exciting or visually interesting, however. Then, if the pursuers came in, you'd need to pan off the characters to the door or film another shot of the door to tell that story. Keeping the depth and having the doorway in shot creates tension and gives you less to shoot.

Artistically, depth provides great opportunities to infuse your shot with colors and shapes. Shallow depth of field will throw some objects out of focus and yield more shot depth. Sometimes depth has gotten me out of trouble. I've filmed in coffee shops or nightclubs and been told by the 1st AD that half of the crowd-scene extras hadn't shown up. We still needed to film a wide shot of the action to establish our busy environment. By utilizing depth, adding a long lens, filling the frame close to camera with supporting artists, and moving behind our characters, we ensured the scene bustled with life. Some walk through frame, others are stationary before walking off; it all helps. One trick is to have some of your supporting artists walk across the frame very close to the camera so they're completely out of focus and unidentifiable. Direct them to walk closer to the main characters off camera, still during the take, before sending them back in across frame. You're effectively turning one supporting artist into two.

Foreground and background are absolutely key in composing a good frame. Try and compose a foreground, midground, and background for every one of your shots, so effectively you're shooting in 3D. Taking advantage of the depth isn't hard; it just takes a little thought on the recce or on the shooting day. Can we move the camera a little to see the doorway, and into the other room over the character's shoulder? Can we position our cast so we film down the length of the long road and not across it? Can we keep our shots visually arresting by shooting through something? Crowds, a fence, a windshield, trees — anything to keep the image alive and busy. In this example we apply depth to a simple medium close-up shot. We see foreground, midground, and background on Caesar (Andy Serkis) in *War for the Planet of the Apes* (2017).

5.5. Keeping the tighter shots alive and busy, like in this shot of Caesar (Andy Serkis) in *War for the Planet of the Apes* (2017).

TELLING THE STORY VISUALLY:
Telling the story visually should be considered part of the fundamentals of filmmaking, but it's surprising how many filmmakers don't do it. Some treat the process like a radio play, with characters speaking their thoughts and narrating events. Ask how your current story beat could be played visually. Is there a look a character could give, or an insert shot to edit, or a juxtaposition of images that can do the heavy lifting for you? If you find a way to tell the story visually, the audience will love you for it; they're actually happy to do the work.

Look at this simple example from *Seabiscuit* (2003). The film tells the story of three characters who've been struggling during the Depression and who've come together to train and race an undersized horse named Seabiscuit. Seabiscuit is feisty and has been trained to lose to bolster the confidence of other horses.

5.6. Visual storytelling in *Seabiscuit* (2003).

Trainer Tom Smith (Chris Cooper) is looking for a jockey who is both brave enough to ride him and a match with Seabiscuit's temperament. At the stables he looks up to see wannabe jockey and stable boy Red Pollard (Tobey Maguire) fighting off fellow stable hands after an altercation. Smith turns to see Seabiscuit's keepers trying to keep him at bay as he rears up and displays his fighting spirit. He looks back again to Red fighting off the stable hands, and we see him make the connection; he might have just found two souls that fit together.

This story beat is all told visually with no dialogue required.

ORIENTATION AND GEOGRAPHY

It doesn't matter where people or things are in reality when you film; it's where the audience thinks they are that counts. Always be asking: *What does the camera see?* Orientation is important to keep in mind when filming and staging. The second the audience is disoriented or confused, you've lost them, perhaps for good. Action films have a tough job with orientation if it's done poorly. The audience must know where the hero, villain, and all other import figures are for tension and excitement to be maintained. Let's say the hero is shooting at the bad guy from across the room and is running out of bullets, but spots a spare gun under the chair ten feet to his right and a doorway he can escape through behind him. First, though, he has to get to the innocent

civilian hiding under the table to his left! Phew! How do we show all that in fast, exciting cuts, and make sure the audience knows who's who and where everyone is? It's important to have a "third eye" that is able to see just what the audience will. Knowing where everyone was when you filmed is not sufficient justification for just shooting mediums or close-ups and hoping the audience see things the same way.

One approach is to put a wide at the top of the scene. Then the audience will know where everyone is for the whole sequence, right? Not quite . . . Orientation reminders are needed throughout the scene, drip-fed to keep the audience in check and aware of the space. *You need to use wider frames, over-the-shoulders, and anchor foreground objects to help place actors in the room.* A wide shot followed by a series of close-ups will be boring and uncinematic and won't cut it. I'm always very mindful of shooting action in a visually impressive location. We need to keep the audience oriented while selling the space that helps define the overall world of the story. It's good to remind the audience of the location with each shot. In the section Making Things Cinematic, we discussed framing wider and using depth to anchor parts of the location to each shot. You may see the doorway just to the left of your character, but if a facial close-up means the camera has framed it out, the audience doesn't.

POSITIONING ACTORS

The director, actor, and DP should discuss actors' positioning prior to each scene. You could ask your actor, "Simon, how do you feel about beginning the scene sitting down before moving to the window?" Hopefully your actor will bring something to the discussion, but it should always involve them and give them a chance to offer input. Staging your actors can have a big impact on the scene. Imagine you have a group of armed thugs racing up stairs to a room to kill our hero. You could cross-cut from the thugs to the hero, sitting in a chair facing the door, gun in hand, waiting. You might get a little bit of tension out of that. However, what if the gun was on the bedside table, and the hero has their back to the door, doing the dishes and laughing with their spouse? Now we have a more palpable tension, since we know more than the character does and they're not ready for the impending threat. This staging also allows the surprise to register better on camera — we see the hero's smile wiped from his face as the action kicks off. That subtle change can make all the difference. Maybe elsewhere you decide to have your actor start a scene sitting down, but after five lines of dialogue they get angry. They can now stand up to visually reflect their emotional change.

Instead of your characters sitting down and talking, perhaps you could stage it as a "walk and talk" where one character is going for their bus or is late for a meeting. Maybe they're in a car? Even better, give the characters a bit of business while they're talking. Having your actors perform an action while talking is an opportunity to reveal character through action. Maybe an office printer isn't working and one character is trying to unplug it or change the ink cartridge. Maybe they're at home unsuccessfully cooking an elaborate meal, or working on a car engine. Giving the characters a piece of business or action within the scene can help elevate it, sometimes by providing subtext or making the characters seem more rounded or fallible. The task at hand might be related to the story or it might be irrelevant — but it can be a wonderful opportunity to make the scene more interesting. Mixing the two enables you to plant an object or device in front of the audience that might seem irrelevant at the time, but could be very useful come the end of the film.

If a character has something else to do (mix cooking ingredients, hammer a nail, eat food, or repair a computer), it allows for physical actions that can then be interrupted. If the dialogue in a scene generates a reaction, stopping actors' physical activity can reflect this visually and reveal something about the characters.

TRANSITIONS

Transitions are something that a director has to get a hold on very early if they want their films to flow. By transitions, I don't mean dissolve effects used in the edit, but how the flow and pace of the film dictate your scene-to-scene movements. It might be a straight cut, or you might fashion a longer lead-up by incorporating a few other shots into the sequence. Done badly, scenes play too jumpy or quickly. Transitions come in two forms; one centers on dispersing emotion and informational flow, while the other jumps around in time and space.

Transitions might be in the form of an establishing shot, or a montage of shots depicting a short passing of time. Imagine cutting from one interior to another to another. An establishing shot or a longer introduction to one of these scenes might be required for the audience to pause, take stock, and absorb the material they've just seen. In addition, audiences like to be slowly guided up to and eased away from an emotion. Cutting this movement short might deny the audience the emotional resonance you're pursuing, sidling filmgoers with a barrage of information they need to digest. Maybe you have a courtroom who-done-it thriller with a scene containing lots of important names and dates. A little breather after a heavy scene like that helps the audience process a lot of information. Shoot character entrances and scene exits. Come the edit, if you find a scene needs a little breathing room before or after, you could use a character's scene exit to buy yourself some transition time before the next scene begins. Let's suppose your script had Character A sitting in their kitchen. Next we see them going for a walk in the park, followed by sitting in a coffee shop. In the edit, you decide for narrative or time purposes to cut the scene of them walking in the park. Now the edit cuts from Character A sitting in their kitchen to them sitting in a coffee shop, and this might play a little repetitively on screen. If you shot them leaving the kitchen and also walking into the coffee shop, even though you *knew* for sure on the day you wouldn't use it, you now have it at your disposal to help break up the edit and prevent the two scenes from playing a little too similarly.

Jumps in time can be done stylishly and seamlessly without resorting to clichés like a close-up on a clock on the wall! Start close on something: an action, such as a door closing or briefcase opening, allows you to jump forward in time ten minutes — or ten hours! Maybe a character brings in a plate of cookies at the end of the first scene. We cut to a close-up of the plate, now empty save for a few crumbs, and then cut to anytime we see fit. *Angels & Demons* (2009) does this very well by showing time has passed from day to night by cutting from a daytime scene to a close-up of a car headlight turning on. This tight shot helps transition us forward in time from day into night. *Cutting to something tight works.* It wipes clean the surroundings in a wonder-fully abstract manner, and the ensuing reveal takes us back to the wider loca-tion or anywhere else we want to be. We can effectively be anywhere we want in time; our close-up has reset the clock. Bigger jumps in time are easier (because different light levels may not need matching), but jumping five or ten minutes later needs to be creatively executed.

This issue can crop up at a moment's notice. Maybe a location falls through, or you have to edit down or remove a scene. Ask yourself constantly: *How will this cut together in the edit?* Anticipate the problem so you can solve it on set, not the edit suite, and avoid the need for an extra pickup shot. Deleting a scene means the footage on both sides of it must cut together well. So you might grab a shot of someone or some-thing to bridge that gap, and you can now show the passing of time or cut around two very similar-looking shots. The problems are endless. The trick is to be aware of transitions and how they play in the edit.

Let's look at a few examples; first, where we jump in time but stay in

the same space, then jump in time in a slightly different place, and finally jump time and space:

In the political thriller *Thirteen Days* (2000) starring Kevin Costner, we have an excellent transition that tries to trick the audience. Costner plays Kenny O'Donnell, an advisor to the President during the Cuban Missile Crisis in 1962. The night before an important press conference, Costner and the President (Bruce Greenwood) discuss the next day's talking points before Costner sees the President out of the empty Oval Office (picture 1). As Costner closes the door behind him (picture 2), we then pan to

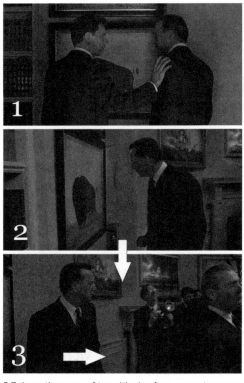

5.7. Inventive ways of transitioning from scene to scene in *Thirteen Days* (2000).

reveal we are now still in the Oval Office but have jumped to moments before the press conference is due to start the following day. In one masterful cut, we have jumped time but stayed in exactly the same place. This is a very clever and creative way of transitioning between scenes. Standard procedure might have seen Costner close the door and cut to an early morning establishing shot of Washington, D.C. before cutting back to the Oval Office.

Sylvester Stallone starred in the remake of *Get Carter* (2000), which featured an interesting transition helped by sound. Stallone confronts a guy who was involved in his brother's death on an apartment balcony over-looking a busy street. As Stallone moves in dangerously close, ready to do damage, we hear the sound of a car alarm in the background (picture 1). We then cut to Stallone leaving the building via the stairwell below (picture 2), walking past the now-dead man facedown on the hood of a car below the balcony (picture 3). We realize that the car alarm from the previous shots was in fact the sound from the shot we're now watching, and has nicely bridged the visual gap. We have jumped forward in time, and the audience must put together what happened and do a little bit of the work. From a production point of view, the film-makers have also nicely avoided

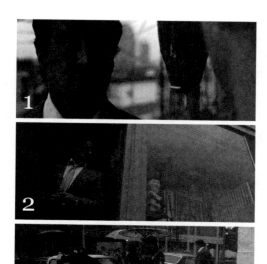

5.8. Creative sound mixing to help transitions in *Get Carter* (2000).

having to throw a stuntman off the balcony and onto the car below. A creative way of not only involving the audience, but saving money, too.

Look at this excellent transition from the ghostly thriller *What Lies Beneath* (2000). At the start of the film, we see Harrison Ford and Michelle Pfeiffer say goodbye to their daughter as she leaves for college. Pfeiffer's character has a hard time letting go. We match cut from them embracing outside the house to embracing in the dorm room. That wonderful cut transitions us from one location to another in an instant, letting us jump time and space while humorously highlighting the mom's inability to say goodbye.

5.9. Finding a humorous way to transition to the next scene, as seen in *What Lies Beneath* (2000).

CROSSING THE LINE, OR THE 180º RULE

Throughout my career, students have worried about and feared crossing the line. They either didn't understand the line or become overly cautious about it. But filmmakers break this rule all the time: sometimes intentionally, sometimes not. The TV show *24* (2001–2010) did it on a regular basis. Ang Lee's *Hulk* (2003) also

crossed the line, even during dialogue scenes. The trick is to know when you should obey the rule and when it's okay to break it. The whole point of it is to help keep orientation, but if you find your angle or edit crosses the line and breaks the rule although your orientation is still intact, then you can let it go.

So what is it? The "line" is an imaginary line that connects two or more people and / or objects. Picture a line running from someone's eyes to where they are looking. A bit like the picture below.

Once we've set up our first angle of the coverage, which will probably be the wide, it is advisable to keep all other camera angles and setups on the same side of the line as established by that first shot. You can cross the line from the wide to the first single shot on your character — but stay on that side for the following reverse shots. Crossing it can impede momentum. My student films featured chase

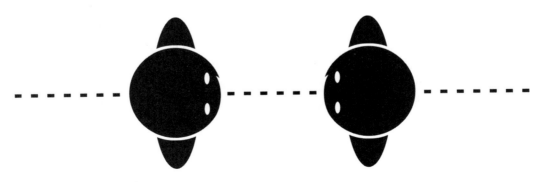

5.10. Line between two people.

scenes that crossed the line all over the place, but we didn't understand why the chases didn't *feel* all that fast. Geography helps your audience orient themselves, so don't confuse them by bouncing your camera all over the place.

Let's take an example. Maybe we have cops chasing robbers in cars. We film a wide of the cars chasing each other from right to left (setup 1), then film the robbers also driving right to left (setup 2) as our first single. Our director mistakenly crosses the line to capture the shot of the cops now driving left to right (setup 3). It now looks like the cops are going in the opposite direction! Maybe in the split-second blink of an eye, the robbers have somehow evaded the cops? No. Even though the cops are going in the right direction on set, what you see on screen is inverted.

It is also possible to cross the line with the camera during a take. You might have a scene with two people talking. One looking right to left, the other looking left to right as normal. Then halfway through the take on one particular angle, you dolly behind the actor's head to their other side. Now that actor is looking to the opposite side of the frame, so the other person in the scene must likewise have their coverage adjusted.

The schedule on a war movie I filmed dictated the first scene shot be an end battle with Allies running and

firing from the left side of the frame to the right. So I had the German soldiers running and firing from the right to the left. All good. Weeks later I shot the lead-up to this attack depicting the Allies preparing for battle. The field used for filming only appeared picturesque from a certain angle, which meant our Allies had to run to battle from right to left of frame — the direction we'd already established the Germans fired during the battle. To have left things this way would have caused the edit to jar slightly; audiences might have been confused which way the Allies were running and, even worse, who was who! To match the previous shot in the field and the forthcoming battle, I needed the camera to cross the line in front of our Allies when they ran in from the right. Those troops then had to run toward camera a little before heading back out the right side of the frame. I shot a low-angle dynamic swoop in front of the first soldier, which corrected my "line" issue and added a cool shot to the movie. When finally edited with the previous footage, the Allies started the battle running in from the left side of the frame and matched my previously filmed battle shots.

Editor Walter Murch (*Cold Mountain*, *The Godfather*, *Ghost*), in his excellent book *In the Blink of an Eye*, lists six factors to make a cut or edit work. In order of importance:

1. Emotion
2. Story
3. Rhythm
4. Eye-trace
5. Two-dimensional plane of screen
6. Three-dimensional space of action

5.11. Creative line-crossing to emphasize an awkward moment between characters in *Safe House* (2012).

What's interesting here is that numbers 5 and 6, which refer to the line and orientation of where people are in the room, come in last. While not crossing the line is very important, you can let it go if other scenic elements like emotion and story are still maintained.

Sometimes the line can be reset. If a character leaves frame on the left, and the next time we see them they are walking directly toward us center frame, that character is now free to walk or look in any direction they please. If they walk or look elsewhere, maintain that newly established direction. You might leave the character and cut to something else entirely. When you return to your character, you have allowed them to move on or walk into frame from a different side.

You can also cross the line for emotional impact. Look at this example from the end of the film *Safe House* (2012) starring Ryan Reynolds. Here CIA agent Matt Weston (Ryan Reynolds) meets with CIA director Harlan Whitford (Sam Shepard) to talk about what was in Reynolds's report detailing the events chronicled in the film. We cut back and forth between the characters as normal, but when Shepard's character suggests something immoral and illegal, we cut to Reynolds's reaction, crossing the line. The editor had a perfectly good angle on Reynolds that we'd seen previously; we break the 180° rule here to establish an uneasy feeling and the sense of something being wrong. The grammar of the filmmaking process is broken to help emphasize a point.

FILMING ACTION — USING THE CAMERA TO TELL YOUR STORY

"Action" could be a fistfight, a shootout, running, driving, chasing, or anything fast paced. Action must firstly always support the narrative and be story propelled. You're in trouble if the story stops while your characters are fighting. The fight has to be the consequence of something, or result in something that will impact the characters and the story. And just like the overall film, even action scenes have a beginning, middle, and end.

Action should be organized chaos, not *actual* chaos. There is a difference. The audience might be watching crazy, random occurrences, but they still need to know what's happening and where — even if the characters don't. *Chaos doesn't equal excitement.* Excitement stems from a sense of jeopardy that the characters are in and that can only be made by clear, cohesive edits that tell that story. Sometimes directors rationalize confusing or incoherent filming and editing as "adding to the chaos," but it doesn't work that way.

There isn't a set way of shooting action; each director has his or her own approach. Solid coverage and orientation count for a lot. And there are other ways to spice up your sequence.

First, set pieces need to be planned and meticulously executed. Action requires that the director is able to think in cuts. Directors unable to previsualize finished sequences will unfortunately miss those small shots required for the story and edit to make

sense. Thus the coverage on action scenes is usually quite immense to stockpile the cuts needed to keep the scene pacey and tell all the story beats.

Shooting some action on a longer lens can compress the image and make things look a little flatter (in a good way). When your actors are subjected to objects crashing down or explosions going off, or they're being smacked in the jaw with a barstool, longer lenses help sell the effect by making things look closer than they are and increasing that sense of jeopardy. The gap between the action and the actor could be many feet away, but shooting from the front on a long lens makes things look like they are right on top of each other.

Long lenses can also help give a sense of speed. If you're panning with a race car or a runner, placing the camera farther back and zooming in for a tighter shot will cause the background to whiz by and make the camerawork feel shaky. All these elements can make someone or something look like they're going faster than they really are. Couple this with some nicely placed foreground detail (a bush, fencepost, or tops of cars in the bottom half of the frame), and you've added both the illusion of speed and a sense of depth to the shot.

Next time you shoot something action-oriented, ask: *What foreground have I got access to? Can I lower the tripod to include some of it? What's the best focal-length lens to shoot this on?*

Whatever the story beat is that needs to be told — no more bullets in the gun; the villain has seen that the doors are unlocked, and the scared woman knows it; the two spies secretly swapped suitcases in the elevator — ask once again: *Is it clear to the camera?* The audience may not process action the way you shot it or the actor portrayed it. What shots do you need to tell that part of the story? It's vital you see it clearly. Miss this point and your scene or film falls apart.

A good tip: *When shooting any kind of action, either the camera or the characters must move. Never use a static shot to film a static character or object.* Either the characters move (turning their head, standing up, taking a step forward), or the camera does. Maybe it spins around them, or pushes into them on a dolly. This particularly applies if a character is watching the action happen off screen. Maybe a fight or shootout is taking place, and the cop's partner (or a relative, or even a full crowd) is watching. Cutting from the fast-paced action with fists flying or cameras whip-panning from action to action, only to then cut to a static shot of someone watching, brings the scene to a grinding halt. So make sure that person moves and physically shifts

their focus in some way to keep up with the other action.

I found out the hard way how important composition is. Years ago I shot a truck chase for a low-budget feature. There I was, on the outside of a camera car racing along the side of a truck at 45 miles per hour! Exciting stuff. But I was framed on the truck. And only the truck. I knew that we were going fast, but the camera didn't see that. I didn't frame in any of the road's white markings zipping by for reference, and there was no foreground or background action. On film the truck looked like it was going much more slowly than it actually was. It might seem obvious now, but it's on these projects that you learn all this stuff. Without any frame of reference, the camera only sees what you tell it to. Just because I knew what we were doing didn't mean the audience would. Not everything translates to the screen.

When filming any action beat, or insert shot you have to be aware of how fast it'll be cut. I learned this big lesson the hard way but haven't forgotten it. The film crew knows who or what is on screen, but when seen quickly the audience might not. To prevent this and aid the editor, we build in physical beats of behavior. Let's say you have a close insert shot of something that is happening fast. Someone being jerked back after being bitten by a monster, a hand dropping a knife, the grabbing of an object . . . The editor will cut into this shot exactly when the fast-paced action whips out of frame. You can't hold on the beginning of the shot for a second or two to let the audience register what the object is or before the character is yanked back, or before someone swipes the object from the shot. This would slow the scene down and look very odd. The solution is to build that time in so the audience can register the action and character choices. If they're grabbing a gun or an object, stage it to be on screen but just out of reach, or have a hand hover hesitantly above before it's yanked away. *This ensures the audience registers the object, with physical and justified action motivating the delay.* Perhaps two people are fighting over a knife and one is demanding the other drop it. With the shot in close-up, dropping it on the first attempt means we cut to it the second the blurry knife falls from frame. So maybe during the struggle with the knife, one character attempts to shake the knife loose but only succeeds on the second attempt. Allowing the audience to clearly see the unsuccessful attempt still plays narratively.

Maybe you have a shot of a character being yanked back by a creature in your horror movie. In order for us to register who the character is, instead of just being pulled from

frame fast, they could be jerked back a little, like they've been bitten and the monster is getting a better hold before yanking him back out of shot. It also enables the actor to play up the horror since we're able to see their face for longer.

FILMING SHOOTOUTS

We've all seen gunfights and shootouts of some kind in a host of blockbusters over the years. Some are truly awe-inspiring, sucking the audience in and making them feel they are right there among the bullets and ricochets. Other times, we feel we're just watching characters we don't care that much about fire at each other without a hint of jeopardy.

What type of film you're making will determine how the shootout is treated and what the consequences of it are. Things play differently in a screwball action comedy than in a serious dramatic thriller. The style of the filming might vary; is it glossy and slick on dollies, or ultra-real, gritty, and lensed with a handheld camera? Directors might also choose to shoot some of the action in slow motion for emphasis and to prolong any visually dynamic action. Whether you use slow-motion or not will be dictated by the style you've adopted. Slow motion is normally chosen for the more fantastic / comedic /

light-hearted action movie, whereas capturing action in real time registers more realistically. The fundamentals, however — action and re-action, establishing who is firing at whom, and where everyone is in relation to each other — will be the same. The 180º rule also helps maintain geography and screen direction, establishing which way the heroes and villains are firing. Like any action sequence, the cuts must be motivated by action. If someone fires, we need to see what they're firing at and if they were successful in hitting it.

In his western epic *Open Range* (2003), director Kevin Costner filmed a lot of shootout action in long takes with a handheld camera to add a sense of realism and forgo a slick and polished approach. He opted for a wider frame in order to see the ground more, and therefore show the distance between characters. On some occasions, the camera operator looks like they themselves were taking

5.12. A handheld camera adding a sense of realism to *Open Range* (2003).

5.13. Letting the action play out in one shot adds impact in *Open Range* (2003).

cover from the bullets whizzing about by having objects in the foreground compromising the frame.

In order to increase realism, the editing in some scenes was also reduced to the minimum. As opposed to many modern action films showing a simple reaction in multiple cuts, Costner and his editors, Michael J. Duthie and Miklos Wright, favored single shots. Like when one of the hired assassins working for the town's crooked boss gets blasted with a shotgun at close range. We see him get shot, fly through the air, hit the wall of the next building, and fall to the ground, all in one continuous shot. To have cut the action into various angles would have lessened its intensity and diluted its impact. We feel that death. Having it cut up into three or four shots would undoubtedly diminish the emotion and the stunt.

Michael Mann's *Heat* (1995) features an over-the-shoulder shot that shows its effectiveness during shootouts. The five shots below depict Robert De Niro during the famous shootout scene on the streets of LA. First, De Niro fires his machine gun in a medium shot; then we cut to an over-the-shoulder shot to see his target; then a cut into the detail shots of car windows shattering and bullets ripping through police cars; and finally, full circle back to De Niro. The geometry is established with the OTS shot anchoring De Niro to the action,

5.14. A powerful over-the-shoulder shot anchors De Niro to the action among all the chaos in *Heat* (1995).

relating his position and distance within his environment. Once that's been established, we can cut to whatever we want. If we were to cut from De Niro firing in the medium shot to the close-ups on cars being ripped full of holes, we would tie the images together — but the impact would be lessened since we don't know how far away the car is or have a wider idea of what's going on. Subconsciously the audience would sense the lack of surroundings.

FILMING WITH MULTIPLE CAMERAS

When deciding between using single or multiple cameras, let the action dictate what you need. Do what works best for you and do not arbitrarily mimic established filmmakers. Ridley Scott (*Alien / Gladiator / Black Hawk Down*) uses multiple cameras even on standard dialogue scenes, as does Steven Spielberg. Directors John McTiernan (*Die Hard / Predator*) and Christopher Nolan (*The Dark Knight / Interstellar*) regularly use just one. Each have their methods and reasoning behind it. Experiment and see which approach suits you best. For time, you might need to use two or three cameras on dialogue, which could compromise your lighting. The way your director of photography lights the wide or medium shot might be slightly different from the way they light the close-up. Close-ups might require more light in the actor's eyes, or be lit in a way that is more flattering that isn't achievable by filming it at the same time as a wide shot. Neither is achievable if you film your wide shot at the same time. A child actor or animal could have their angle captured, as well as that of their scene partner. This way, if they do something special or unexpected, every take will match seamlessly. Shooting comedy is another area where more than one camera might be useful. On action or stunt scenes where an effect or move cannot be easily repeated, multiple cameras offer more opportunity to capture all the angles. In general, if you have two cameras and are struggling to find a place for the second one, you don't need it.

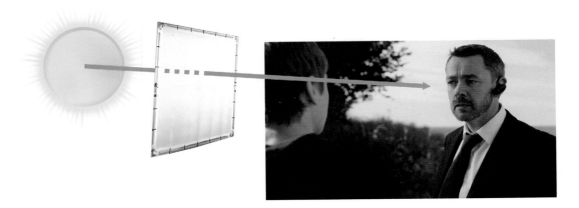

4.22. A breakdown demonstrating lighting daytime exteriors.

4.24. A breakdown demonstrating lighting daytime interiors.

4.25. A breakdown demonstrating lighting night exteriors.

4.26. A breakdown demonstrating lighting night interiors.

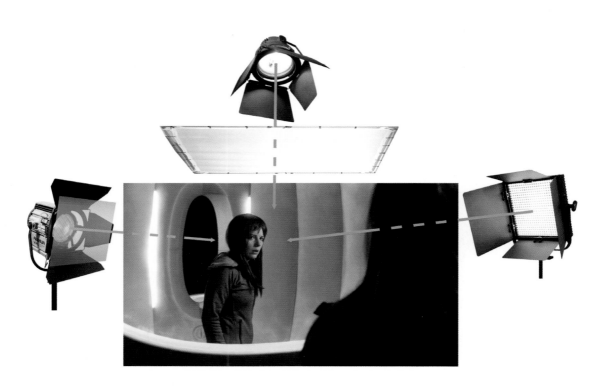

4.27. A breakdown demonstrating lighting night interiors in a studio.

ORIGINAL LOG FOOTAGE

S-CURVE AND VIGNETTE

BLEACH BYPASS LOOK

BIG COUNTRY LOOK

8.9. The original log footage, an S-curve and vignette applied, and a couple of look presets from a grading session.

9.7. Keep an eye out for green spill if an actor is too close to the green screen.

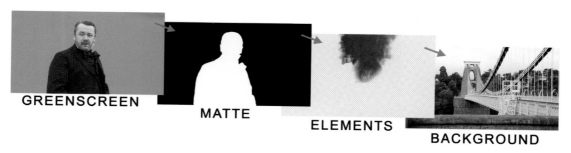

GREENSCREEN   MATTE   ELEMENTS   BACKGROUND

9.13. The complete process from green screen to final composition.

CHAPTER 6

FIREARMS, STUNTS, AND FIGHTS IN YOUR BLOCKBUSTER

"Everybody says CGI is the death of stunt people, but it's not. They still need people to physically perform; otherwise, you turn into a cartoon."

— VIC ARMSTRONG, STUNT COORDINATOR, 2ND UNIT DIRECTOR

Now we're really getting to the fun stuff; but also the most dangerous. Pay extra attention. Get this next part wrong and you could find yourself arrested or in prison! This is a time where you need to enlist expert professionals to help you. Remember my story about running in the bank with a blank-firing firearm? Don't let that be you . . . Okay, enough warnings, let's talk firearms, stunts, and fights. Any and all types of films can feature these aspects; they're not just reserved for your action blockbusters.

ARMORERS AND USING FIREARMS

If you are using any sort of firearm or weapon on set, you must employ the services of a registered firearms dealer or armorer. The supply of these weapons, real or imitation, must be via a firearm dealer or licensed supplier. When filming with armorers in the USA, research each location's requirements, as they do vary from state to state (and sometimes from city to city). Each state conforms to federal guidelines and is allowed to create additional regulations as they see fit. In the United Kingdom, the Firearms Act of 1968 reads: *It is an offence for any person to have in their possession a firearm, shotgun, or ammunition without holding a valid firearm or shotgun certificate or certificate of registration and complying with its terms and conditions.* Section 12 of the Firearms Act allows filmmakers to hold weapons in their possession when a supervising film armorer is present, however.

Armorers are highly skilled professionals and can offer more than just the firearms themselves. They make sure the cast and crew are safe, and that the actors use weapons consistent with their character or role. They can break down the script and offer suggestions to make the action more realistic too. They can liaise with the prop department to ensure that the prop versions of the weapons being used are the same as the replica or blank-firing firearms being provided.

There are three different types of guns used in films:

1. Real ones that have been converted to fire blanks (a cartridge or casing containing gunpowder but no bullet). To use this type of firearm in the U.K., an armorer must have two licenses: a

Registered Firearms Dealers license (RFD), and, in order to handle "banned weapons," the Home Office Authority to Possess Prohibited Weapons (also known as the Section 5 license). This includes handguns, machine guns, etc. In the state of California, USA, for example, the equivalent is an Entertainment Firearms Permit, or EFP, that must be issued in order for firearms to be rented or used by prop masters in the film and TV industries.

2. Rubber guns. These are used for stunt work and do not fire. If an actor or stunt person is falling, running, or throwing, or anytime where it could be dangerous to have the real thing in hand, a rubber version is a much safer option. They're sealed and molded with no moving parts so are great for characters just holding a gun.

3. Replica / deactivated guns. This would include airsoft / BB versions

6.1. Naomie Harris in *Skyfall* (2012).

or guns that can no longer be fired. The film unit is only allowed to be in possession of these guns for the duration of the shoot.

As listed above, besides using blank-firing guns, BB or airsoft versions also offer realistic replica weapon replacements. Both BB guns and airsoft versions are primarily used for target practice and training, but also have an extensive role in film and TV work. Both systems use either CO_2 or gas propulsion when ejecting their small steel BB or plastic pellets. You don't need to actually fire anything to film the *appearance* of firing, of course. For the most realistic-looking replica weapons, airsoft look more like the real thing. Try to find ones with blowback action, where the top slide moves back, simulating the blowback recoil. Blowback makes things look very real, especially if you're adding shells and muzzle flashes in post-production via visual effects. Read more in the visual-effects chapter.

There are many hazards blank-firing firearms present. First off, you have the noise. Blanks, used to simulate noise and shell casings being ejected, are loud, especially if the weapon used is a semi- or full automatic, and the noise will echo for a while in an enclosed space. Earplugs are used in these instances. Debris, discharge, and flying objects (like spent cartridges ejected from the top of a gun) are all things to be aware of. Gases emitted

from shell casings can cause fires and injuries like cuts and burns. Blanks can even be fatal. An armorer can pull the plug on a scene if they deem it to be unsafe.

When filming, if the actor holding the gun has to aim or fire it at another actor, the armorer will make a visual mark on the wall behind the character under threat using tape or chalk. This gives the actor with the weapon something to aim; they never actually point the gun directly at the other actor, although it will look like such on camera. The target is made for consistency and is not just a random point; in later takes, an actor's concentration could wander and his aim could accidentally drift toward the other actor.

For safety, the scene is rehearsed with the guns empty of any blank ammunition. Before shooting, cast and crew are fitted with earplugs; the sound of blanks being fired can reach 160 decibels. Any unneeded cast or crew might also leave the set. A drape or riot shield is also placed over or near the camera to protect the operator and assistants. Optical flats (clear filters) are also placed in the matte box to protect the lens from any debris. After any final checks from hair and make-up, the armorer loads the gun before handing it to the actor. When a gun is ready to be used, the armorer will say "weapons hot" to the actor and surrounding cast and crew. This let's everyone know that

6.2. A blank-firing Glock with magazine removed and slide in locked position.

the gun is able to fire when the trigger is pulled. Once "cut" has been called, the armorer is the first person back on set to take the gun off the actor, make it safe, and reload it if necessary. The armorer shows or "proves" it to the actor, visually letting them see that the gun is now empty. Between takes, the gun is either locked away or stored safely, with its top slide portion in its locked position, and its magazine removed.

It is the responsibility of the producer to ensure the production has all the right permissions and certificates for everything firearm related. He or she needs to consult with the hired professionals, the police, and the local film office. A risk assessment will need to be carried out and kept on set detailing hazards and procedures, and what controls are in place. The police can't take chances if a member of the public reports guns or other weapons out in the open. You know it's a toy gun, but the old lady who lives down the street doesn't. If she sees it from a distance, then you might be getting a call from the boys in blue; likewise, a member of the public who hears a blank being fired may call the police, who will then have to respond. Keep police informed to prevent misunderstandings. In the U.K., if filming in a public area, the police will have to be notified and the producer can secure a Film Weapon CAD (Computer-Aided Dispatch) reference number and a point of contact within the force. If anything goes wrong or the police inadvertently turn up on set, you can produce your certificates and reference numbers. The CAD number is forwarded to the police switchboard team. If they get a call from a concerned member of the public, they can see that at the address the sighting has been reported, there is a known film crew present with the proper CAD number assigned. They will still have to show up on set, but to confirm you are indeed a film production and not a criminal enterprise. Police forces have their own security restrictions for productions in terms of the transportation of weapons and their use on location. The Met in London, for example, has its own film unit dedicated to helping filmmakers.

WHAT IS A STUNT?

Stunts can be exciting and fun to shoot — but can also be very hazardous. A stunt is anything that would be dangerous for your actors to perform on camera, so professionals are hired to double for them. Stunts can range from performing in dangerous environments, falling from high places, fight scenes, being set on fire, crashing cars, jumping out of planes, or generally being thrown about. This is why the stunt and special effect departments work

hand in hand; their work is often very closely related. They're both there to create the most impressive and dangerous-looking images they can, but in a safe way.

Any stunt work requires lots of rehearsal to make sure the action is performed safely and to match the actions of the character the stunt person is doubling. Camera operators filming the action need to know what the complete action will be to make sure they can frame it correctly as well. An excellent safety guideline regarding filmed stunt work is to not add any finishing touches while the camera is rolling. It's these last-minute touches or additions, when the stuntman decides to run a little faster or jump a little higher, that cause accidents. There is a difference too between physical acting and stunt work. All actors can roll about and be thrown to the floor. A stunt is a dangerous piece of action that requires an experienced professional, or for an actor to be suitably trained. Actors may undertake slightly dangerous stunts themselves, but eventually a pro must take over. Actors like to say "I did my own stunts," but unless they are adequately trained to perform that action safely, it's more physical acting than stunt work.

From a general filming perspective, with any special effect or stunt gag it is always advisable to shoot the action a little wider to make sure you capture it. You don't want to be caught framing the action too tightly to add a sense of chaos or danger, only to miss the full impact of the stunt, or even the whole stunt itself.

To be a stunt person in the U.K. and get on the British Stunt Register, you have to prove you can master six different disciplines. Some choices include: rock climbing, swimming, high diving, horse riding, martial arts, gymnastics, driving (competed in five rally-driving competitions), and motorbike racing, among others.

Each set will have a stunt coordinator or intermediate whose job it is to plan and oversee any stunts performed by the stunt team. For safety, the stunt coordinator does a risk assessment, planning for all possible outcomes. Stunt people are trained professionals with years of experience. Knowing the main elements and hazards to look out is good, but no one can anticipate all possible variables affecting a stunt.

Stunts can cover many different areas, but let's look at a couple of the more popular ones.

HIGH FALLS:

We've all seen movies where the villain falls to their death, or maybe the detective's partner gets killed when the bad guys throw him off a roof. What must the stunt team consider if your script calls for a high fall? The stunt person can fall into either an airbag or a layer of cardboard boxes. Airbags are good if you plan on shooting a scene many times, since the rest time is fast. Boxes, however, need to be repositioned after each fall; over time, they won't be as safe. If you only plan on asking your stunt person to fall once or twice, boxes are the most likely choice — but not for anything over 100 feet. As a general rule of thumb, if your stunt person is falling 10 feet, you need one layer of boxes; if you go up to 20 feet, you'll need another layer of boxes. The stunt team will also make sure there aren't gaps between the boxes when setting them up; otherwise, the stunt person could fall through them. For safety, the corners of the boxes are sawn off or bashed in to remove their hard edges, which are dangerous to land upon. The stunt person can fall into them in various ways, too. They might fall headfirst and flip over, thrusting their body to ensure they land covering as much of the airbag or boxes as possible. They need to make sure they don't pencil into them feet-first, greatly increasing the hard landing.

The stunt coordinator and their team will recce the location beforehand. There are a number of environmental factors and other variables to control, and you need to factor in how many takes you can allot for a stunt. For example, a little rain might turn boxes soft over time; this is

6.3. Stuntman Neil Chapelhow trains for a high fall stunt.

a big safety concern. Wind will affect the distance objects travel. The higher a stunt person is, the farther out they will fall. If falling on fire, an airbag must be used (not boxes, for obvious reasons), and the bag must be coated with fire-resistant gel.

Stability of the take-off platform is also an issue. From where are they jumping? Is the platform firm and uncluttered, or moving and soft? Can the stunt person see the landing area? If the stunt person is performing the lead-up to the high fall alone, they have a little more control over things than if they're being thrown by another since they can launch them-selves. These are just some of the hazards to look out for when preparing this type of stunt.

There are several different ways of falling. A "faceoff" or "header" is a traditional fall; a "suicide gainer" is a backwards somersault; and a "seat drop" is a low-level fall. The stunt person trains and rehearses in comfortable clothes to perfect the action before getting into costume at the location. They are familiar with all the elements of a safe landing. They're easy to perform in sweatpants, but in full costume as a medieval knight is a different story.

From a camera perspective, the filming angle is paramount. To make things look bigger and higher, a lower, wider angle is best, and this of course frames out the airbag or boxes. An OTS from the top is also another possibility, but the operator needs to make sure the shot frames out the bag at the bottom. The editor does the rest, cutting to onlookers before cutting to the body on the floor, if required.

FIRE STUNTS:
To preserve safety, two or more auxil-iary stunt people (in addition to the stunt person) must be on set for any

6.4. Stuntmen in a full-burn fire stunt from *Saving Private Ryan* (1998).

sort of fire stunt. The additional stunt people will have fire extinguishers (regular and backup) and a fire blanket, as well as other fire supplies to cover all possibilities.

There three different types of burns:

Partial burn — Arms and legs on fire.
A half burn — Covering half the body.
Full burn — A full-body burn.

When performing fire stunts, a fire-resistant, translucent gel is spread over the areas that are to be ignited. The gel reduces the heat and allows the stunt to be performed without burning the stunt person. For the full-body burn, the stunt person wears a mask with a gap for the mouth and eyes, as well as a race suit, the same ones worn by Formula 1 drivers. The suit is made of a fire-resistant material called Nomex, and is soaked in the translucent gel the night before. For fire gags, filming inside or in darker environments is preferable because the fire plays better on camera. If you're filming outside, shooting during the magic hour is best; aim for when the sun has gone but there is still a light in the sky. This way you're not fighting exposure issues, with the sun washing out the fire. Framing wise, medium shots work well when filming fire stunts; it is easier to see the person and their reactions. Too close and you'll frame out the fire.

Stunt teams understand the genre you might be working in, and can adjust and tweak a stunt to match that style. There is no "one size fits all." Directors can present the story beats they want to see, and then the stunt coordinator can offer their thoughts on how things can be executed. It's a nice mix of inputs from the stunt coordinator, the director, and the DP.

To get the best out of your stunt coordinator and stunt team, you can always pre-vis the shot, showing them exactly what you're looking for. They can then offer their input and refine it, practicing and rehearsing that idea. Stunts are their life, and they know how to best shoot and stage their stunts. To get the best from them on camera and sell their stunt, request and listen to their input.

The stunt world is forever developing and moving on. From just stunt-doubling actors, stunt people now also sometimes have lines and acting parts. The stunt person should be able to act enough to portray a character's pain or fear during the moment of the stunt. It's now quite possible to replace the face of the stunt person performing the death-defying stunt with that of the actor. Stunt people will be the unsung heroes of the action blockbuster for some time to come.

FIGHT COORDINATORS

First off, just knowing how to fight in real life does not make someone a good fight coordinator or performer. Fighters are trained to damage; fight coordinators are trained for safety. Some moves might be technically correct and in accordance with a particular fighting style, but look awful on screen and require adjustments for the camera. A certain flamboyance

must exist for the camera to see the punches and kicks work in a fight. It's also a dance between the performers and the camera operator. The coordinator also has to have an understanding of timing and editing. Fights can be heavily cut up in the edit suite, so sequences can be designed to accommodate that. Camera coverage of the fight needs to be planned rigorously in order for the sequence to work well. I build in a few moments of "respite" to punctuate the fight. This allows the action to slow for a brief moment so the audience can catch up. Otherwise, there is a tendency for everything to just fly through frame fast and blurry. We as the crew might know what's just happened, but will the audience see it play on camera?

A good fight coordinator will break the script down and suggest ideas that work for the characters, the location, and the story; the fight should be a product of these three elements. A fight between two co-workers in a factory setting will be a lot different than two trained martial artists going toe to toe. One will be messy and uncoordinated, and one will be slick and assured. Just make sure you don't mix the two.

SHOOTING FIGHT SEQUENCES

I've been filming fight scenes since I was 11. Back then the punching sounds were made by an off-camera friend hitting their palm whenever a fist was thrown. Early on we noticed the camera had to be in a certain position to give the impression of the punch connecting without seeing the gap. Then we progressed to "hitting" each other with frying pans and garden chairs . . . This was all good fun, and good practice for things to come. Any film can feature a fight, whether it's a high-octane action flick or an intimate relationship drama. There is a difference between seeing people fight and clearly following a fight on screen. Excitement and jeopardy only come from the second one. Editors and directors know what the shots are, but if they're cut too fast or poorly framed, can the audience follow them? *The Bourne Supremacy* (2004) style of fast cuts and dizzying fight moves is often emulated but not executed correctly, earning blame for the current crop of poor and unclear scenes in action movies. Shaking your camera while in close-up to add a sense of "chaos" is not the answer.

During dialogue, normally one person speaks, then the other. A fight sequence can to a certain extent be shot in a similar manner: one attacks and one reacts. Choosing the shot sizes when shooting action is just as important as when lensing dialogue. Too far away and it isn't that exciting; too close and the swinging arms and reactions are all out of frame. Unlike dialogue, you can't really film

a fight sequence using a wide master shot followed by two singles for the *entire* scene. Your actors will wear out filming the entire wide shot; by the time you get to the closer coverage, they're exhausted. Safety concerns and fatigue could well preclude filming a long wide, and the punches probably won't "sell" since that singular camera angle allows the audience to see the gap between fist and face. Some short fights can be captured in one master without singles, but they must be meticulously executed.

A fight coordinator should rehearse with the actors well in advance of shooting. Time spent on set arranging and planning a fight will cost you money.

Fights should be broken into filmable units consisting of 3–5 fight moves per chunk. Any more than that and you may need a new camera position or lighting setup to sell the hits connecting. The camera operator will have to be on the move for the punches to work, too. Filming fight scenes presents a nice little adrenaline buzz and keeps the operator one step ahead of the action. If the operator is late getting into position to capture the second or third hit, the punch might lose its impact. Look at the frame below: we see the camera wasn't quite high enough and in the correct position, so the impact is lost behind the attacker's shoulder.

6.5. The impact of a punch can be lost behind a shoulder if action is filmed incorrectly.

Block the fight a few times at half speed, then when ready, turn the camera on and film. Once you have one angle in the can, change the size of the shot slightly rather than just shooting another take of the same thing. You could pop out wider or go in a little tighter for a slightly more frantic feel, giving you a little something extra come the edit.

Shoot the majority of the action in medium shots, with both a two shot and an OTS on each fighter. Any closer and you risk visual confusion, with arms and bodies just flying through frame. Look at this image below as an

6.6. If the cameraperson frames too tight, body language and threat are missed.

example. The medium shot of the fist and arm flying through the frame is nicely framed. If the camera operator were to more tightly frame the attacker, as highlighted, we'd miss all those intimidating body gestures and just have the blurry fist whip through frame at the end.

Since we can't see the gap between fist and recipient, framing over-the-shoulder and on a slightly longer lens also compresses the action a little and helps sell the impact clearly. Take a look at the image below:

So shoot one side, then the other, and on each shot place the camera over the fighter's shoulder. Sometimes shooting the reverse angle necessitates a complete relighting of the scene. You might shoot in one direction, then go back and pick up the

reverse angles of the whole fight. This would also entail make-up and costume changes since blood might have appeared more prominent after a particular hit. At a certain key moment in the fight when the geography is all set up, you could punch into a tighter shot to emphasize things: a leg kick or finishing move, for example.

The audience needs to see what is happening and where. *If they have no sense of place, they can't enjoy the action, and the sense of jeopardy is lost.* We can only be impressed with what we see and feel. Seeing an onscreen blur and hearing a few punchy sound effects gives the *impression* of a fight, but has zero impact on the audience. Again, shots for each section of the fight might be broken down into

6.7. Fights captured on a longer lens compress action, selling the impact.

two OTS singles and a two shot / wide (if geography needs to be re-established), and will find a natural end to that sequence before starting again on a new section. These little clips can be united to constitute the completed fight sequence. Wide shots still require energy; going too wide might lose the visceral nature of the fight. Sometimes the action is very fast, so if you can give clues to aid orientation, like showing more of the space, then the audience instantly knows where they are and are free to enjoy the action.

When lighting for action, I'm happy to let some small lighting niggles go for time. Each shot will probably be on screen for seconds, perhaps only frames, so the audience's eyes will be on the action, not that slightly

hot practical light in the top corner of the frame. You can waste a lot of time trying to remove a hotspot or reflection when only the crew would know what it is.

It's good to overlap and thoroughly cover the action to give yourself options during edit. You don't want to find yourself cornered and forced to use the one bad shot or hit. I've shot fights where the third punch out of five wasn't good and the hit didn't register. The director liked the overall take, so we looked at the OTS shots of the same series of hits. From this new angle, the same third punch was blocked or somehow flared, so we didn't have it from a good, clean angle. For us, as it will be for you, it was a creative call as to whether we moved on and let it go or went back and

6.8. The 4-fists rule shows the gap between the fighters.

captured it. The choice is yours, but note each hit and don't get caught up in the excitement and adrenaline. You don't want to be in the edit and forced to use a bad shot.

For safety and to avoid accidents during fights, apply the 4-fists rule. Make sure the hand on the end of the swinging punch is four fists away from the recipient's face. Experienced fighters can work safely using a 2-fist gap. With hits to the stomach or other areas, you can't apply the 4-fists rule, but padding can be worn to cover the area of impact, and techniques how to safely pull a blow that makes contact can be learned.

To sell a punch to the face or body, the reaction is more important than the action. As long as the person getting hit sells the impact, it's buyable to the camera. If the action is excellent but the reaction isn't there, it won't sell, so good acting is paramount. It's as much an acting exercise as it is a physical and technical one. Fighters should constantly use eye contact and "check in" with each other so they know when it's safe to throw a punch and can react properly. If this link between the actors is lost, you could find yourself too close or too far away, and then you risk either an accident or an unbelievable hit.

When cutting your fight together, it's good practice to show the attacker and their incoming punch first, and then cut to the hit and reaction. In the edit, do not cut on the exact moment of impact between the two shots; cut to just before the impact itself. The audience can then actually see the hit on the shot of the recipient. Cutting to the reaction exactly on the hit of the outgoing shot might dilute the impact. This is because in the moment of the cut we are presented with the reaction, so by the time our eyes and brain adjust to and process the new shot, it's all over. We may see the punch, but it carries less weight. Try it next time you're cutting a fight scene.

Another editing trick is to cut your fights using the drop frame method. The editor deletes the frame of action just before impact, making the image jump forward and accentuate the hit.

You can also use the camera's frame rates to sell the action. Maybe you're filming an action sequence where the performers aren't that fast or confident. You may decide to shoot the action at 22 frames per second, thus speeding up the action when played back at 24 or 25 fps. It would be very subtle, but enough to make the fighters and the sequence better. You could even shoot at 12 fps and have the fighters actually make contact, but slowly and safely. Then when played back at the normal speed and frame rate, you have an actual contact hit real time on screen. Slow motion can also

6.9. *John Wick* (2014) shows how fight scenes can be captured in longer shots.

be used for emphasis or excitement, but it comes down to the tone and style of the film. Adding slow motion to an otherwise real world or gritty action film might not work. Maybe you decide that your action and violence play better in real time. The choice is yours.

When shooting fights or action, beware of fatigue. With fatigue comes impaired concentration and heightened safety concerns. People get injured and accidents happen. In addition to safety, dips in concentration may also cause continuity issues if actors forget their movements.

Finally, look at two different approaches to fight sequences. *John Wick* (2014) sees Keanu Reeves fighting some assassins invading his home. A longer scene with a

particularly impressive ending shows Keanu taking out the final assassin in one shot. We start on a wide and slowly push in as Keanu finally kills them. We don't cut away; we sit and watch them both struggle until it's over.

Now look at Liam Neeson take out a guard in *Taken 2* on the next page. One neck-snapping action takes nine cuts to tell this story.

So it's not all about fast cuts, close-ups, and shaking the camera. Too many edits might mean the fight choreography is not presented optimally. The awe of the scene comes from seeing all the action clearly, and perhaps holding on an angle for a series of moves rather than having a cut for each one. Then you're able to give the audience the adrenaline ride they paid for.

6.10. A simple action in *Taken 2* (2012) broken down into numerous edits.

CHAPTER 7

SPECIAL EFFECTS IN YOUR BLOCKBUSTER

"It's really not about the tool; it's about your imagination and what you bring to the film and the shot. The tool doesn't matter."
— DENNIS MUREN, VISUAL EFFECTS SUPERVISOR

Effects fall into two categories: Special effects refer to any practical, on set, in-camera work like snow, wind, and rain; pyrotechnics like explosions, bullet hits, fire, or smoke; and any animatronics. Visual effects refer to anything done digitally: sky replacements, CG ships and monsters, and even digital actors! We'll look at visual effects in a later chapter. There is of course a crossover between the two areas as rain, snow, fire, and explosions can all be done digitally too. Which department you assign to do the effect for you will come down to your resources, contacts, and budget. Each area has its pros and cons. Some visual effects save time and offer complete control

of their timing and deployment, providing you more options later on. The con is your actors have nothing to react to, so the scene could look fake or poorly executed and it might end up costing you more money. The right choice will come down to what you can afford and what you have at your disposal.

Even though you're not actually doing the effects work yourself, as a director, camera operator, producer, editor, or whatever your role might be, you need to be aware of the best ways to interpolate these features into your production. You need to know where to place your cameras, what speeds the cameras are running, how to cut the shots, and what sounds to dub over them. Also, from a producing point of view, we're into health and safety, timescales, and similar expenses! I won't talk about how to create these effect elements; that's where your hired professional comes in. But I will address how to best incorporate these elements into your work.

I've had the pleasure of using both practical and computer graphics in my films. There's a lot of fun to be had from both. I've experienced the adrenaline rush before a large, one-take practical effect is set off, and a similar feeling seeing a photo-real CG image and knowing you're about to pull the wool over the audience's eyes. And it all starts with a line in the script.

My first experience with using pyrotechnics was over 20 years ago, filming an actor running away from a huge explosion for the finale of a movie. I contacted a special effects professional to help me film, and a lot of lessons were learned that day. The edit clearly revealed how much I had to learn about camera placement. Since I didn't understand image depth, my cameras were a little too far to the side of the action. A still photographer was on the scene, and his action shots caught a better angle on the explosion than mine did. This bugged me, and I had to work out why. He positioned himself in front of the actor running and shot on a longer lens, compressing the distance

between the actor and the explosion. This suggested the danger was right behind the actor rather than the reality of the action being at a clear, safe distance. I had my cameras on a wider lens. Consequently, the explosion looked both farther away and a lot smaller. Also, the edges of the fireball in the still photographer's image were just touching the sides of the frame and looked better. This was before you could crop an image without a drop in quality. Lessons learned.

Using special effects in your work can be fun and exciting. Even though you'd bring in a professional to do the heavy lifting, special effects of all kinds will affect most other departments. As a director, director of photography, or editor, you need to know the best way to capture and show the effect. That's what we'll look at in this explosive chapter.

TYPES OF EFFECTS

Special effects cover a wide range of areas: pyrotechnics, atmosphere (rain and snow), miniatures, breakable glass and windows, and weapons and firearms. Special effects crop up in all types of film work, from action films to dramas, and they don't just refer to the spectacular elements; they can be as simple as a campfire or a hand breaking through glass.

PYROTECHNICS

Pyrotechnics encompass sparks, bangs, explosions, bullet hits, squibs, smoke, flares, fire, and fireworks. You MUST secure the services of a professional for this work; you put yourself and your team in danger by doing otherwise. Not only are pyrotechnics dangerous — fire, debris, and flying objects — they also take time to set up and cost a lot to execute.

Let's look at a few different types of pyrotechnics.

FIRE:

Fire can feature on film in any number of ways from a burning house to a campfire. From a camera perspective, pyrotechnics or any fire gag can be quite bright, so keep an eye on your exposure too. It can quite easily look overexposed at its core so you will need to stop down your aperture to prevent this and make it look nice and saturated. This may mean you need additional light to bring up the exposure of the surrounding area of the frame. I've found that fire plays best on screen if the color temperature on your camera is set to 4300K to produce that fiery orange look. If filming in a studio, your set walls will need to be built from a fire-resistant board to prevent your set from burning out of control. From a safety perspective, the fire department should also supervise. Fire can be depicted using flame bars placed behind furniture or hidden around the set, or placed directly in front of the camera to serve as foreground and

7.1. Flame bar.

give the impression of fire engulfing the scene. Flame bars are connected to a gas supply and regulator that can control the size of the flames.

EXPLOSIONS:

Explosions come in many shapes, sizes, and colors, depending on their cause. It could be gasoline cans, a gas leak, air pressure, or any number of things. It could be a big, black smoke cloud, or a bright orange fireball. If you need to blow up part of a building, the effects technicians might load a firing funnel full of chopped-up cork and soft debris. When a fireball rips through a window or corridor, we see parts of the walls and building as well as the explosion. Cork is used because it's soft and wouldn't do much damage were it to

land anywhere or hit anyone. Safety is paramount when dealing with these elements. I once secured the back-yard of a trucking company to set off an explosion during a final shootout scene. We had our two actors running from a barrel that would explode behind them. Seconds before the cameras rolled, our effects technician gave one final safety check around the area and discovered a bunch of old nails scattered and hidden among the dusty dirt on the ground. If the explosion had gone off, our actors could have had sharp debris raining down on them.

As mentioned above, I shot my first explosion too wide and it looked small, but this was back when you couldn't manipulate an image that much. However, with today's cameras

7.2. A pyrotechnic explosion.

it is best to go a little wider with your choice of lens to ensure you capture all the effects on display, particularly when shooting pyrotechnics. You now have the ability to crop and reframe your finished image. However, you can't go wider in post if you cut anything out of the frame during shooting. When filming "one time" effect shots, most directors employ multiple cameras. Capturing the effect from as many different angles as safety and budget will allow gives you lots of options in the edit. Some cameras can film in slow motion, at 120 frames per second or thereabouts, capturing the intensity of the action very well. I once erred shooting an explosion gag when I had a set built for the exterior of a hotel window that was going to be blown out. The window set was constructed with the hotel's exterior walls on both sides. I thought the explosion would rip through the window and shoot out far away from the hotel. However, once on set, I realized something my inexperience had cost me. The explosion would only be as big on screen as the set would allow. This might read as obvious, but I had a vision in my head although I only had half the resources (and experience) to execute it, and everything got blurred together in my mind. The edge of frame was the edge of the set. I wanted the explosion to fire out wide beyond the set with the sky as a backdrop — but to frame wider you have

to frame higher too. This was where I ran into problems. What I should have done was make sure the set was bigger, with hotel walls to the side *and* above and below, giving me the wider shot necessary to see the whole effect I had in my mind. The explosion might fire out fifty feet from the window, but that's irrelevant the second it leaves frame. In addition, one of the side walls could have been dressed to look like the edge of the building rather than just a window in the middle. I could have shot off the set and seen sky, enabling me to frame even wider and capture the fifty-foot-long explosion. The shot was eventually discarded. Lesson learned again.

SQUIBS:

A squib is a small explosive charge that is strapped to an actor's body or placed in a wall to simulate a bullet hit. Like most special effects, they can be pricey, currently costing between $35 and $65 (£25–£50) per squib. A metal plate is strapped to an actor's body with the small explosive charge rigged to the plate. A blood bag is then taped over the charge, ready to explode when the charge is fired. This can take time to set up, as the cable for the electrical charge has to be run down the leg of the actor and out to a firing box. Make sure the costume department has a few extra outfits on standby or you'll be limited to one take to get the action right. When squibs are rigged in walls

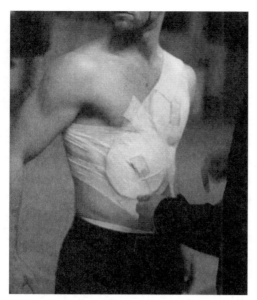

7.3. Explosive squibs being rigged to an actor.

and doors, small holes are drilled into the surface and the charge and debris are then placed on top. The hole is then repainted or wallpapered over the top so the charge can rip through, firing out the dirt or wood and creating the illusion of a bullet hit. Some forethought must be taken here to ensure you can make holes in the walls of your location. A cheaper and quicker alternative on the market is a small pellet gun. Compressed-air units can fire small breakaway pellets with a charge and dust particle inside. Just like paintballs, the pellets break on impact, and the effect is a small spark or dust pocket.

ATMOSPHERE

Your script might call for your actors to be kissing in the rain, or walking to church on a snowy Christmas Eve . . . you can't sit around and wait for those conditions. Even if you did, you wouldn't be able to control it. That is where special effects come in. If you have wind, rain, snow, or any type of weather in your script, make sure it definitely has a reason for being there; these elements can put a big hole in your budget. But if they are essential and you have the resources, they can also be a lot of fun to work with. A few things to consider:

Wind — Wind machines can be very large in order to produce the desired effect. They also need steady power. Any production sound recording, if you do manage to record it on the day of shooting, will only be a guide track. Wind machines, essentially giant fans, are very noisy.

7.4. Wind machines ready to create a storm.

Rain — Rain machines also require power for the water pump, and any camera equipment will need proper housing and protection. Consider the source of the water and consult with your special effects professional. The

7.5. Falling rain created by using rain machines.

rain has to come from somewhere, so a source of clean water must be transported or be available at the location. You must backlight rain in order to see it properly. If you had a scene with rain and one shot was backlit but the reverse was not, it would appear on camera that it was not raining on the reverse angle. You're dealing with water on set, so electrical hazards must also be taken into account. See the image above of a rain machine in action.

Snow — There are as many as six different types of special effect snow, depending on what your shot requires and what end result you are aiming for. Maybe you need to cover a field, or have your actors walk through

falling snow, or have a frosty sprinkle over your cobbled street. In contrast to rain, snow must be front-lit to see it play on camera. Snow may also require clean-up after the shoot. You can pay some effects companies to do this for you, but it could take another day or so to get your location back to its original condition.

MINIATURES

Miniatures are small models of sets, locations, or vehicles that are filmed when it's not possible to use a full-size version. Maybe the full-size version can't risk damage or simply doesn't exist. A miniature might be constructed if a large location, object, or effect is impossible to achieve through location filming. It's a good option if building an object full-size is cost-prohibitive. With CGI quickly gaining popularity, visual effects are sometimes an easier route to take — images can be changed and altered. The bigger the miniatures are, the better they film; the interaction between light and model is more realistic. But fire and water don't scale down on camera very well, so if your miniatures must be blown up or put underwater or the like, it's best to make them as big as possible. This way you have a better chance of the shot looking real. Our eyes are very good at perceiving depth, so models are sometimes shot through a haze of smoke to add that layer of atmosphere we'd be looking through in real life. To achieve this, models are sometimes shot in a sealed studio so smoke can fill the space and its levels can be maintained. Ridley Scott was not initially happy with the look when filming a model ship landing on a planet for *Alien* (1979). So he opted to film it only with a low-resolution video camera and then only see the model via the images displayed on the monitors the characters were looking at in their ship. A creative way of solving the issue when a model didn't quite look right.

BREAKAWAY PROPS

If your scene calls for someone to be thrown through a window or have a beer bottle broken over their head, or involves any type of dangerous glass or material, you will need to bring in a professional. "Breakaways" are molded from sugar glass that breaks very easily under very little force. It can still cause injuries, though, so it is very important that care be taken when using such specialty items. Like most props, they can be very expensive; the budget might only allow for three bottles to be broken, so you only have a set number of takes to get the action right.

FINALLY, A NOTE ABOUT EDITING

When editing any type of visual or special effect, there is a tendency to hold on every last frame to make sure you get your money's worth on screen. But this only slows your edit (and the film) down. *Be ruthless. Cut away from a shot fast and leave the audience wanting more.* The best approach is to treat it like any other edit or action. Once a shot has served its purpose, cut. The shot could be your first time doing effects work, or devoured most of your budget, but it will have a much greater impact if you are uncompromising in its presentation. The same principle applies to long slow pans around your gorgeous set or location; all you're doing is slowing the film down as you show off your effect or set. Do what editors do best: CUT!

CHAPTER 8

EDITING YOUR BLOCKBUSTER

*"The editor builds the house with the bricks
the director has given him, and then they both
sit down to decide how to decorate it."*

— TERRY RAWLINGS, EDITOR

ADVENTURES IN THE EDIT SUITE

Many filmmakers find editing to be the most fun part of a project. You're seeing everything you've worked so hard on for the past weeks, months, or years come together. The pieces become a movie before your eyes, all in the comfort of a warm edit suite! Everything you do in pre-production and production anticipates the edit. Every little shot, glance, insert, or second camera angle exists to make the edit smoothly coalesce. Films are made in the edit suite.

Why do we edit? We edit for continuity, to make sure a character's actions match and cut seamlessly from one shot to the next, suggesting the action is happening for real and unfolding naturally before our eyes. Secondly, we edit for effect. We want to induce a response in the audience and manipulate their emotions, be that joy, terror, excitement, sadness, pity, or love.

Scenes can be cut and recut over and over to tell a different story and give a scenario a different meaning. The story is told in cuts; glances, close-ups, reaction shots, and pauses help the audience follow and understand what is happening. Like music, it isn't just the notes you hit, but the pauses in between that give an edit its power. An editor who worked in TV news cut one of my early drama films. His first assembly cut out all the important pauses before and after dialogue. This gave the film a very literal meaning and changed the feelings the actors and myself wanted to convey. It's the pause before someone speaks that might let us know they are lying, or the beat between words that shows the character's internal struggle. Cutting out these important pieces can drain your film of its emotion and subtext.

Knowing *when* to cut is the most important skill to master for an editor. In order to do this correctly, you must know the footage and the story well, and have a solid grasp of emotion and the human condition. Cuts are sometimes required to keep sequences alive, so the coverage must be gathered to provide the necessary material to the editor. On the flipside, editing and overcutting can kill the rhythm of a scene. Sometimes one needs to step away from the keyboard and let the wider shot play out in its entirety. *Knowing which is which on any given scene is the secret.*

Whether you cut your own material or work with an editor, being able to separate yourself from the footage and the emotions surrounding filming day is paramount. A shot you love might have taken hours to set up, but prove to be unnecessary. Or you dislike a shot because it's a bit soft focuswise, and the actor kept forgetting his lines, but it's required to help the story makes sense. A separate editor

many not have these impressions, but you know you will if you're cutting your own film. Director Michael Bay (*Transformers*, *The Rock*) says that every film has "turkey shots." Shots you hate but must be kept in the film for the story to work. Only you think it's a turkey shot; it will fly by the audience since they'll be engrossed in the scene.

THE PSYCHOLOGY OF THE EDITOR

An editor has to possess a third eye, one able to see everything from the audience's point of view. In fact, any good director needs this ability too. The ability to clear the mind of any influences from the set. They need to see the raw footage with a fresh, objective pair of eyes. Creative leads may discuss, take apart, and develop a story, character, or plot point many times during writing and production. But all that matters is what the audience sees and when. I term this the "Mom factor." I ask, "Will my mom get this? Will that information translate off the screen and into her consciousness?" Of course, my mom just represents the everyday audience member not privy to inside lingo on technical film terms or the meaning of a certain shot. My mom doesn't know if the coverage is missing a shot or if a shot is an homage to some throwback movie from the 50s . . . She'll just say the film was boring, or she got confused, or she didn't understand it. The editor has to see the film from my mom's point of view.

A superior editor trusts his or her intuition and gut feelings. 99% of the time, they are correct to do so. They must remember those feelings weeks or months down the line when the scene or film doesn't mean what it used to. They may no longer feel the same fear or emotion, but the audience will on first viewing. Cutting comedy is a good example of this. A funny line or scene ceases to be funny after repeated viewing, so an editor might wrongly tweak and trim humorous content, overlooking their initial gut reactions and (innocently) incorporating only what is registering as funny at that moment. The trick is to realize this and get out of your own way. Action or fight scenes work similarly; the editor or director may know a scene inside and out, and they trim extensively to make things "more exciting" and frantic. However, all they are doing is taking the edit past the point of cohesion. When the editor and director subsequently watch it, they still see the previous environment and action. These omissions will confuse the audience, not make the sequence better. *Don't ruin a scene by trying to make it perfect.* Always ask: What will the audience see?

BEGINNING THE EDIT — RUSHES / DAILIES

"Rushes" or "dailies" are all your original, unedited footage. Now that your film is shot, the edit can begin. This is also the stage where certain thoughts and questions emerge. *Did you get everything you needed on the shoot? Will that shot of my star actor cut with the reverse shot? Did I cross the line when the villain walked in the room? The film is nowhere near what I was hoping for and will be a complete mess . . .* You may remember shots you dropped because of time constraints. You will also watch shots in isolation and think they represent your whole film. But 95% of what you watch in dailies won't be used.

Have a solid idea about how your film should be cut. Hopefully, you've given yourself enough material and coverage to adapt to new ideas and change things too. Strong coverage is the key to superior editing; the editor can't cut what hasn't been shot. Coverage isn't simply "collecting" footage and dumping it on the editor, but having an idea of where and how you want the pieces to go. Alternatives do exist should your planned route not work as well as you'd hoped.

You might watch a take and not like it very much, although on set everything looked fine! Did someone sneak into your edit suite and replace all your good takes with mediocre ones? What happened? On set your adrenaline is pumping, or you're tired, or your mind is focused on your crazy schedule. You might see a take slightly differently a few days later from the comfort of your edit suite.

Beginning the edit is always an exciting and nerve-wracking time. Part of me can't wait to see my movie come together, and the other part is apprehensive a scene won't work as well I'd hoped. One thing that I have learned is that most of the time edits can be saved with some creative tweaking. You just have to get to that point.

Before I actually cut, I review all the takes and angles and make notes on each shot for a scene: "Wide shot 32.2 — Good performance, Dan; wind noise at end." The "32" refers to the shot number, and the ".2" refers to take 2. So not only have I familiarized myself with the shots, I know which ones are good and have moments I can use. I certainly note any magic. When I come to a particular line, I can look at my notes and see that there are three superior performances. Then I decide which delivery best fits the tone of the scene. Directors shouldn't be too quick to call "Cut!" after a take. Occasionally a take needs to go on one more second, or even a few frames longer. Were I to opt for a closing dissolve or a slightly extended emotional beat, I wouldn't have the

shots since I called "Cut!" too quickly. The operator is already lowering the camera down from his or her shoulder.

Good questions to ask are: *Why are we cutting here?* and *What does this angle give us that the old one didn't?* Just because the camera operator pulled focus at that point in the shot doesn't mean you have to use it. Just because the camera craned down on that line doesn't mean you have to see it.

Key moments in any wide shots will become apparent, and they really tell your story, becoming the backbone of the edit and building from there. A good rule of thumb in post-production is: broad strokes first. Start laying down shots to see if the rough assembly works as a whole. Then you can go in and refine, trim, and finesse. This applies to editing, visual effects, music, and sound mixing too. I've seen editors agonize over cuts for their first two shots; at that rate, they'll need a few years in post! The broad strokes approach generates an overall feel, and fast. Very often, that first stroke will be just what you're looking for. Then you can then go in a layer deeper and finesse the areas that need it. Then you can go in deeper still. By starting and agonizing over the small details first, you forfeit a sense of the whole — and that shot or scene might be cut anyway! And you've spent three hours tweaking frame edits. I like going back to review a scene or edit a few days after it's been cut. It's immediately apparent if it works or not, and you can tweak the performances accordingly. I review alternate and even previously dismissed takes for different glances or looks; you never know where something valuable might surface.

A famous expression in writing and editing is to "kill your darlings." In other words: cut out something you love. That gorgeous shot of the sunset, that nice (expensive) crane move, and that amazing (and even more expensive) visual effects shot all need to be treated the same way as any other shots in the movie. If it slows the film down, damages the pace, or is redundant in any way, CUT IT. It's hard. You know how long it took to get that shot. But every edit must serve the scene and overall film.

JUXTAPOSITION

Juxtaposition is defined as having two elements side by side. Each individual element has its own meaning, but when two are placed together, a new, third meaning is created. These elements could be two shots side by side, or a shot and a piece of music, or even a photo and a newspaper headline. The two shots cut together tell us a story; adding dramatic music changes that story. The same shot and some comedic music offer up a

different story altogether. The audience puts the two elements together and creates the third idea. Editors use juxtaposition all the time to help move a story along and create emotional weight. It's a proven, tried, and trusted technique in the grammar of film editing.

A good example of juxtaposition is the finale of the thriller *Silence of the Lambs* (1991). The finale of the film sees heroine Clarice Starling (Jodie Foster) ringing the bell of a house as she looks for information on a serial killer who is holding a woman captive. A SWAT team has also arrived at another house, and we see a police officer dressed as a flower-delivery driver ringing a doorbell too. Juxtaposing the images of Clarice and the empty house uses the audience's awareness of film grammar to suggest that Clarice is ringing that house's bell. The sound edits also inform us; we see her press the doorbell and hear it ring when we cut to the interior of the house. Then a shot of the deliveryman / officer ringing his doorbell is juxtaposed with the serial killer's house, and we hear that bell ring. This suggests to us that the SWAT team is right outside the serial killer's place and are about to apprehend him. When the doors finally open, Clarice is in fact ringing the door of the serial killer's home, and the SWAT team are at the empty house. We weren't lied to; it was us, the audience, who made the assumption through traditional juxtaposition of the images. This twist then kicks off the finale of the film.

CUTTING ON ACTION

Back in the early 1900s, directors like D. W. Griffith established the basic grammar of film and knew the psychological power the "cut" held. Griffith made films such as *Birth of a Nation* (1915) and *Orphans of the Storm* (1921), and he fashioned the "invisible cut." Cutting on action helped audiences engage with the story and not be distracted by a choppy edit.

Cutting on action means cutting together two shots, perhaps a wide and a medium, or a single close-up and a reverse single close-up, in the moment someone performs an action. This could be when a character takes a drink, opens a door, turns to walk away, or gets up from a chair.

This gives the audience the subconscious impression that all events are unfolding in real time. To cut back to a wide shot *before* someone performs an action could suggest that the camera knew something was imminent, breaking your scene's reality.

Sometimes, to optimize pace and character, you might need to let the action play out in its entirety and not cut to other shots. To cut on an action just because you can would be a mistake and could damage the pacing. You need to rely on your gut feeling about the scene and what it requires.

Sometimes the widely adapted and conventional approach isn't always best, however. In the thriller *Blown Away* (1994), the villain, Tommy Lee Jones, may have planted a bomb in hero Jeff Bridges's home, where his wife and daughter have recently arrived. As they pack away their groceries, director Stephen Hopkins cuts to extreme angles to suggest

8.1. Creating tension by *not* cutting on the action.

where a bomb may be planted: a high angle of a light switch, a close-up of a stove knob . . . We cut to these shots a few seconds before the characters perform any action to suggest that these switches or electrical appliances might cause the bomb to go off. The audience jumps ahead of the characters, creating palpable tension. If we were to cut to the light switch on the action as the character turned it on, there wouldn't be enough time for the audience to make the connection, thereby removing any sense of threat or tension. So, like most of filmmaking, there are reliable, proven methods of doing things, but also times when the opposite may be the best option.

EDITING ACTION

Editing action can be a lot of fun. It's challenging: you're trying to keep things involving and thrilling for the viewer, but also maintain a sense of geography and orientation.

Your director should have given you enough material to make the sequence work. The footage you have hopefully adheres to conventional film mechanics and grammar, like the 180º rule and consistent screen direction. Lots of coverage keeps action scenes fresh and exciting. If you're going to have a pickup day, it might well be because of a few necessary shots missing from a sequence. Cutting action doesn't necessarily mean filming guns, chases, and explosions, but anything with fast-moving scenes or objects: race cars, a sporting event, or a fast-paced comedy sketch.

One of my favorite yet simple edits in an action film is in *Die Hard* (1988). Bruce is hiding in a darkroom, and a terrorist who knows he is in there appears and turns on the lights. They flicker a little as the terrorist walks towards Bruce, to whom we cut as

8.2. John McClane (Bruce Willis) has been discovered in *Die Hard* (1988).

143

the rest of the lights flicker on. This cut binds the two together so we know definitively they are in the same room and only feet from each other! The action is only seconds away from kicking off. My heart always races at that moment, every time I watch it.

When editing action, make sure you connect the characters to the action, or the spectacle won't mean anything. During that chase, invasion, big fight scene, or final sports game, the audience needs to see characters' reactions. Are they concerned, happy, scared, full of wonder? Cutting to a few close-ups of the characters and their reactions gives the big, expensive spectacle more significance since we're now experiencing it through their eyes. Don't spend too long away from your principal cast. Cutting to a few extras or stuntmen in peril is good for two or three shots, but return swiftly to your lead actors.

To ensure audiences follow the action, you may be required at some point to show that a character is looking at or has seen something. The editing has to tell this story for you; it's not enough for the actor just to look at the object or person, we need to connect the two. Among all the excitement, the audience might well have missed it. The sequence may consist of two shots cut into a little 3-shot montage. We have a medium or close-up shot of the character looking off camera, then a shot of

what they're looking at, then back to the first shot. The middle shot can be a wide, medium, or close-up, but it's good to frame this action more centrally, as a point of view (POV), to distinguish it from the other, more objective angles being used. The action is thus tied to the person seeing and experiencing it. This little rule keeps the audience in sync with the story. Look at this example from the James Bond film *Casino Royale* (2006). Bond is chasing the suspect through a building site during the opening of the film. After crashing down from a big height, Bond glances up just in time to see where his suspect is going. Without it, Bond would get up and the audience would ask, "But how does Bond know where he went?" Slipping in these few shots

8.3. Daniel Craig as James Bond demonstrating a familiar editing device.

tells us Bond spotted where he was heading. It seems small, but it's imperative that you capture these shots and edit them accordingly. The juxtaposition tells the story.

Take a look at this nice, simple sequence from the thriller *Ronin* (1998), starring Robert De Niro and Jean Reno. De Niro is about to fire a missile at a car they're chasing, and these shots give us place, screen direction, detail, geography, and action / reaction. The wide shows us the car and De Niro (picture 1); the OTS shot of De Niro shows him getting into position, and the car in front gives us distance (picture 2); the medium on De Niro shows him lining up the missile (picture 3); the close-up on the

trigger shows us he's fired (picture 4); the close-up on the missile's muzzle flash offers the action (picture 5); and finally we see the resulting re-action as the car in front is hit (picture 6). All of the shots respect the screen direction too, with the action and De Niro framed from the left to the right-hand side of the screen.

INCREASING SUSPENSE — SUPERMAN VS. THE MAN OF STEEL

Now we come to suspense. Let's compare two examples: *Superman* (1978) and *Man of Steel* (2012). Both feature scenes of Superman rescuing

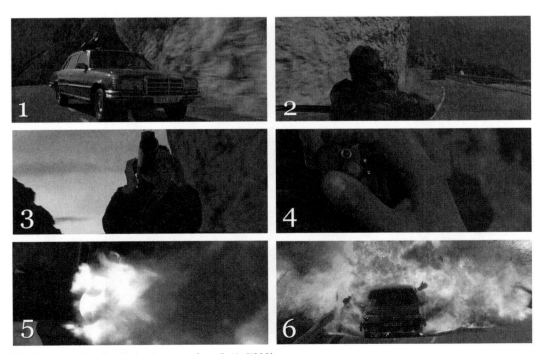

8.4. A simple and well-edited action scene from *Ronin* (1998).

145

people in jeopardy, but only one allows the audience time to ask questions of the action. This can make a world of difference.

In *Superman*, Lois Lane boards a helicopter from the top of the *Daily Planet* office. On take-off, the landing skids get caught in some rooftop cables, and the helicopter spins out of control before coming to a stop on the side of a skyscraper. Lois slips and falls, hanging precariously off the helicopter door, about to fall to her death.

In *Man of Steel*, Clark is on a fishing boat when the skipper diverts their course to rescue people trapped on an oil rig. Let's look at the two timelines. In *Superman*, we witness the helicopter accident and see the public watch in horror for a solid 2.25 minutes *before* Clark comes bumbling out of the *Daily Planet*'s doors to investigate. We are then teased for another 35 seconds by editor Stuart Baird as Clark tries to find a suitable hiding place to change

into Superman and save Lois. That's a tantalizing three minutes of setup and building tension the audience must endure before Superman even flies into action. Then that tension can be released. Director Richard Donner and editor Baird delay Clark's awareness until the last possible moment, then delay us again. This succeeds because the audience has been allowed time to ask two important questions: "When will Clark find out about the helicopter accident?" and "Will he get there in time to save Lois?"

In *Man of Steel*, Clark is made aware of an oil rig fire and then immediately disappears off the boat. We cut to the riggers inside trying to find a breathing apparatus. We are in their company for a second before the door is ripped off and Clark appears. How much time passes from Clark's awareness to the rigger's rescue? 17 seconds. This 17 seconds isn't long enough for the questions above to be asked, and

8.5. Superman (Christopher Reeve) saves the day in *Superman* (1978).

therefore the tension cannot build. And we find out about the oil rig fire when Clark does, not in advance. In *Man of Steel* the audience is simply *watching* the events unfold rather than being *emotionally involved* in them. *Superman* maximizes the sense of jeopardy by affording the audience time to ask these simple questions.

WHEN THE JIGSAW DOESN'T FIT — EDITING MISMATCHES

When covering any sort of action that is repeated from various angles, unless you have shot the scene with multiple cameras, you may find an actor's actions simply don't match when cutting from one angle to the next. It's going to happen, since when actors are in the moment, they often do things slightly differently from scene to scene and take to take. Mismatching can cause any number of headaches for the editor.

The most important element is the emotion of the scene, not the exact position of the actor's body. When the audience is fully involved in the characters, they seldom notice mismatched cuts. Bad edits can also be hidden by sleight of hand and movement elsewhere in the frame. Look at this example from *The Nice Guys* (2016). Here we see the joining frames from a scene at the end of the movie where Russell Crowe and Ryan

Gosling are at a bar talking. The two characters are in different positions; Crowe's cigar and Gosling's cigarette both change positions between shots. Crowe is even looking in a different direction. This cut works because the moment we cut to the second shot, Gosling leans back and distracts us; in a split second, this movement causes the two shots to coalesce in our brain so it appears they match.

8.6. Editing mismatches don't have to jar, as shown by this example from *The Nice Guys* (2016).

I've had edits before where someone has their hand up by their face while talking, and in the next shot it's down by their side. I found a point to cut into the second shot when arms were in motion, and this "movement," when cut next to the previous shot, was merged to resemble the hand lowering! It shouldn't work, but it does.

Here's an even bigger mismatch. Look at Harrison Ford as the titular character in *Indiana Jones and the Kingdom of the Crystal Skull* (2008). Indy's head is looking to the right; then

8.7. Indiana Jones (Harrison Ford) moves a little between shots, but did we notice?

in a cut he's facing forward. It didn't seem to bother Steven Spielberg or editor Michael Kahn, so maybe you can get away with it too.

WHEN IT'S JUST NOT GOING RIGHT . . .

Have you ever had an edit where a film or scene just kind of sits there? Something not engaging, not enticing, no fun? I've had those, films that work as an assembly and tell a story but are dead to look at. Editor Walter Murch in his excellent book *In the Blink of an Eye* offers good advice: If a scene isn't working well, the problem might not lie with the scene at hand, but instead be that something important hasn't been set up earlier. So the problem with Scene 10 might actually be in 7, where something is missing.

If the problem doesn't lie in the setup but the scene itself, it's time to come at it from a new perspective. Ask

yourself: What is this scene about? What is the information we're trying to get across here? When you have a point of focus and a point of view, you approach the scene with a fresh perspective, one that perhaps doesn't support that first shot you've chosen.

Also, I've found that a whole scene can sometimes feel slow or give the feeling of something not quite being right purely because of a single shot or one overlong edit. *That one edit in the wrong place affects and infects everything that comes after it.* If that shot happens quite near the front of the scene, that's why the scene "feels" funny. It's not that the whole scene feels slow; it's that one particular shot is slow and tarnishes all that follows. If an edit seems sluggish, first try to find the offending long shot or repeated shot before hacking away at the good stuff.

THE POWER OF A TEMP SCORE

We'll discuss temp score a little more in the music chapter, but it also relates to cutting. There's a moment when your sequence is first matched with music, either from a temp score or from what the composer has provided, and your film gets a whole new lease on life. Dramatic scenes become more emotional; action sections become more suspenseful; comedic scenes become even funnier. Watching the film or scene with a musical score may confirm it works and has value, were you doubting such. You need to get the first assembly to a desirable place, but rather than finessing the picture first and adding music later, perhaps introduce a temp score now and see what happens. Let's consider this comment by *Gladiator* director Ridley Scott: "I think it's dangerous to [look at the film] without any temp. Some editors say you should look at it dry. I don't agree. I think you should look at it with whatever you need to make it work. Because otherwise you can discard a lot of material if you're looking at it dry that you may have been able to use." This is an interesting point, and I have made this mistake in films I've cut. I've cut shots believing a scene is too long or too slow, but placing music over the top of it had a bonding and lifting quality that connected the shots in a transformative, unifying way.

COLOR CORRECTION

Color correction, sometimes referred to as grading or timing, takes place after editing, and is a very important part of the finishing process. Color correction and grading are wonderful tools for enhancing or technically improving your blockbuster. On most projects you would have a dedicated colorist to do this job, but on smaller-budget films, this role might fall to the editor. You can color-correct in your NLE of

choice, or in your compositing software or a dedicated grading and finishing package like DaVinci Resolve. Every package adjusts luminance and image color, although their technical language or control placement may vary. You correct the image for three reasons:

To balance the colors and brightness on shots in the same scene that were perhaps filmed at different times or places but must match each other. Maybe the sun went in, or the lighting was slightly different on the second day when you grabbed those last few shots. Grading now means you can make everything look like it was filmed at the same time.

For the "look" of the film. We've all seen films that have a certain color palette to them. Maybe a blueish tint, or dark and gloomy, or warm and fuzzy. Give your film a desired look to help tell your story.

In order to meet the technical standards of the broadcaster or distributor. Films and programs are quality-controlled to guarantee the colors and brightness levels are within legal parameters. If the whites are too bright (sometimes referred to as "clipping"), the grade can bring them into line. Or maybe some of the colors are bleeding into each other, which too can be detected here.

When filming your blockbuster, you can choose whether you shoot with a log profile, or in the more traditional, linear "Rec. 709" color space. Log

8.8. A grading suite.

(logarithmic color space) is designed to give the DP and grader a large dynamic range between the darker and lighter areas of the imagery. Of course, you don't have to shoot log, as filming in the Rec. 709 linear color space still has a good dynamic range; log, however, offers you a little more latitude. But if you have the option and a good grader on board, then shoot in a log profile. Log files are captured flat with the contrast and saturation low, maximizing your options when you correct and grade your footage.

The first or primary color-correction pass is about matching the blacks, midtones, highlights, and white balance from shot to shot and getting a good overall exposure. The colorist uses the secondary pass to look at skin tones and isolate particular areas of the frame to be adjusted. More sophisticated grading programs such as DaVinci's Resolve or FilmLight's Baselight offer tools such as "power windows." A power window is a masking tool where the grader can highlight part of the image by drawing a small mask or outline around it, only affecting the areas within that space. So if the whole image is lit and balanced well, but the doorway area is a little bright, this area alone may be fixed without affecting the overall image. You can even track the movements of an actor's face and brighten or darken them as they move.

Once balanced, you can then give the image a particular "look." Maybe you want it high contrast, low contrast, magical-looking and diffused, or raw, gritty, and color-desaturated . . . the choice is yours. Your film's look rests upon the creative choices of the grader, the DP, and the director. There is no right or wrong, just individual tastes.

When color correcting and giving your picture a look, be mindful of forcing something onto the film that doesn't work. I made a film once where I knew I wanted a certain look in the grade. When I got to the edit and applied it, my gut told me instantly it didn't work. The look applied was too gloomy for the subject matter. It may have looked okay elsewhere, but not on my film. The trick is to listen to this gut feeling when something isn't right. Don't force something through just because you *knew* it had to look that way ever since you began thinking of the film.

There are a number of approaches to creating that blockbuster sheen. One is to apply an S-curve. Adding a couple of points using your curve tool subtly makes blacks darker and pushes the highlights. It makes the image a little more contrast-laden, a look that is sometimes associated with film stock. It's called an S-curve because adding the two points (one a third up from the bottom, another a third down from the

top) creates a shallow-looking *S* on the controls. By moving any points along the curve, you're remapping the input brightness or color levels of the source footage to new output levels, making objects brighter or darker. A vignette is a tool that slightly darkens the edge of your image and forces your eye to the middle of the frame, making the subject "pop." You might also desaturate the colors a little. Color presets are also available in NLE and grading packages, which can give your footage a particular look or shine or even be used to emulate film stocks. These presets can then be tweaked and adjusted to suit your needs. These same looks can be achieved from scratch working off the original footage and adjusting the color and luminance levels, but the presets offer different options and a nice shortcut. Of course, these are just a few of many approaches that can be used and played with. It all depends on the film you're making and the story you're telling. Refer to image 8.9 (color insert) to see examples of the original log footage, the shot with an d vignette applied, and several different looks.

Finally, the director of photography should also be present during corrections since this part of the process is an extension of their work. They might be using the grade to correct a few things they didn't have time to change during shooting, or to make sure the overall look being applied is in keeping with their original vision.

CHAPTER 9

VISUAL EFFECTS IN YOUR BLOCKBUSTER

*"All art is technology. That's the
very nature of it. The artist is always
bumping against that technology."*

— GEORGE LUCAS, VISUAL-EFFECTS PIONEER / DIRECTOR

I've always been fascinated by effects movies. From my *Star Wars* (1977) and *Back to the Future* (1985) viewings as a kid through the subtle use of effects in *Forrest Gump* (1994) and *Cast Away* (2000), I've been trying to pinpoint how this magic got made. What sleight of hand did the magician use? Computer Generated Imagery (CGI) gets a bad rap when used in films that are all spectacle and no heart. It is just one of many filmmaking tools, and the CGI isn't necessarily the reason a film doesn't work.

Some visual effects are easy and some are incredibly hard. My artists and I have completed gorgeous shots in minutes; others take days or even months of working, like slowly building up a matte painting for it to be on screen for just five seconds.

The world of visual effects has moved on as technology has improved. The artist's creative visions have forced the technology to keep up. A visual effects shot requires an enormous amount of work, talent, and skill from the artist and other people involved. Pioneer directors Robert Zemeckis, George Lucas, and James Cameron use these tools to create the images they envision, telling their story without reminding audiences that they're watching visual effects. Audiences might also fail to notice the heavy visual effects and CGI work in dramas like

Pride and Prejudice (2005) and *Atonement* (2007). That gorgeous midnight moon that Lizzy Bennet looks up at? CGI. That setting sun and painterly sky above the fields in *Atonement*? CGI. Those crowd scenes in the marketplace? All of them, and many more.

HISTORY

The first computer-generated scene to ever appear in a movie was the "genesis sequence" in *Star Trek II: The Wrath of Khan* (1982) wherein a moon transformed into a lush green planet. It was created by the effects house Industrial Light and Magic (ILM), who'd already done hundreds of effects shots on films such as *Star Wars* (1977) and *Raiders of the Lost Ark* (1981). ILM later produced the first fully CG character

in *The Young Sherlock Holmes* (1985). The technology continued improving and birthing new software programs and approaches, and 1991's *Terminator 2: Judgment Day* proved a breakthrough. The liquid metal T-1000 supervillain used new, cutting-edge technology extensively. The biggest advancement in CG occurred two years later when the T. Rex walked the earth again in *Jurassic Park* (1993).

HOW CAN YOU USE VISUAL EFFECTS?

I started messing around in the world of visual effects years ago when I made a World War II film. I taught myself the compositing program Adobe After Effects and began seeing what could be achieved. A total of seven visual effect shots were

9.1. The T-1000 (Robert Patrick) as seen in *Terminator 2: Judgment Day* (1991).

completed for that film, including a CG fighter plane and bullet ricochets. My next film progressed to 33 visual effect shots involving a CG snowflake, falling snow, and sky replacements. My PC at the time could barely handle all that processing!

Use tools to aid story points without drawing attention to them. It can be fun to sneak these shots past the audience. Some visual effects can save you in the edit, too. Sky replacements are just that: an artist replaces the sky. Maybe you had blue sky and nice puffy clouds all day while shooting, but the last few shots occurred after the light had been lost and don't match the others. That's where the computer can help you. Maybe you had a perfect take performance-wise, but a lighting reflector crept into shot for a split second. Here the computer and a talented artist can help you by painting the reflector out. *Young and new directors alike should study visual effects extensively to know their full scope and potential.* Knowing you can paint a boom pole out or change a sign in shot means fewer compromises on set. Visual effects can be very costly. But they can also be done very easily and very cheaply using readily available desktop software. It depends on your goals. The desktop software and state-of-the-art devices to run it were once available only to high-end

visual effects companies, but are now accessible to everyone. The computer power on your laptop is bigger and better than what was used to create the CGI in *Jurassic Park* back in 1993. A talented artist still needs to know the software and have a good eye, but resources out of reach years ago are now at your disposal.

What are visual effects commonly used for? We've mentioned a few, so let's list some more:

- Digital set extensions
- Face replacements
- Green screen work
- Digital pyrotechnics, smoke, fire, explosions, sparks, gunfire
- Painting out unwanted objects or people
- Blood spatter
- Adding CG models such as ships, planes, monsters, or buildings
- Creating 3D environments: cityscapes, water, planets
- Sky replacements
- Combining groups of actors in one shot to create large crowd scenes

Check out this split-screen image showing the before and after a sky replacement has been added.

9.2. Replacing the sky using visual effects.

START BY SEEING

Great visual artists of any kind start by seeing. Firstly, look around your environment and really see the world in front of you. This is the same for any camera people looking to improve their lighting, or any visual effects students looking to get ahead in the CG world. Observing allows you to see how objects react to each other and where they fall in various settings. Look at the way light changes as the sun goes down, how shadows fall, the qualities of reflections on cars and windows. Note how haze in the sky filters more over objects as it moves farther away, toward the horizon. See how light interacts with metallic surfaces, paint, and wood finishes. Look at the atmosphere and how smoke spins and whirls, and how fire moves (and its colors). We have seen these things before, but haven't necessarily looked closely. It is here that the best artists are born. They know how to reproduce what they see when creating the illusion in visual effects. Sometimes big explosions or spectacle are more easily created; they pull the wool over the audience's eyes more than the invisible everyday effects we're all used to seeing.

PROGRAMS

To achieve these visual effect shots, there are a number of programs on the market that can help. Some packages do everything you require, while others are more specialized and only perform one particular function.

Compositing programs:
- Adobe After
  Effects — Layer-based
- Nuke — Node-based
- Flame — Node-based

3D design and animation:
- Autodesk 3ds Max
- Cinema 4D
- Modo
- Softimage
- Maya

Other image-manipulating software:
- Adobe Photoshop — Photos,
  backgrounds, texturing maps
  for 3D models
- Smoke — Editing and
  visual effects
- PFTrack — Camera tracking and
  match-moving software

Most programs have an established import and export pipeline or workflow with other programs to simplify exporting from the NLE (Non-Linear Editing) software or 3D animation package into the compositing program and back out to the NLE.

TERMINOLOGY

Let's take a look at some of the common terminology and elements found regarding visual effects. They took me a while to learn and understand how they interact. You'll learn

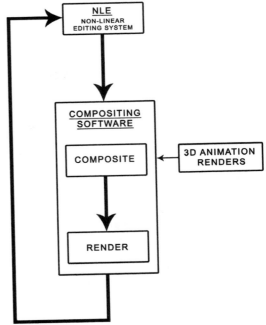

9.3. The visual effects pipeline from editing software to compositing software and back again.

the most seeing the process in action, from location or studio shoot to visual effects suite. Any directors, producers, DPs, or editors out there should familiarize themselves with these terms so they are able to speak the language of their visual effects supervisor or artist when on set.

Composite — The final image containing all the elements in a shot. The background plate with the actors, the CG dinosaur (or whatever CG model you may have), and the CG smoke effects all added together, ready to go back to the editor and be placed in the film. All of the individual layers are squashed down to create a single file clip, as though the scene were shot as one. Compositing programs such as Adobe After Effects or Nuke can do this. Anything can be placed on top of your video layer, but to have things behind it would involve cutting your subject out either with green screen or rotoscoping work.

Green / Blue screen — Objects or actors can be filmed in front of a green or blue screen as foreground elements, and then composited into a background plate. The green / blue part of the image is removed in the computer

9.4. The final composite fully rendered.

9.5. The actor and green screen element.

by "keying," leaving behind an empty space to be filled with other images. The green screen process allows a "matte" to be created.

Matte — In the older days of film processing, a "matte" was created by having part of the image blocked off, usually by a black card or paint, to prevent exposure in that part of the frame. It could then be optically composited with another image, allowing two images to be combined. Before it was done digitally, film images were combined using optical compositing. A matte is an opaque image (not transparent) providing control over which areas of the frame we discard and which areas we keep. The green screen process and roto-scoping can both achieve a matte that can then be used for compositing.

Keying — The process of removing a particular color from a filmed image. Usually blue or green screen, but can also be black if filming pyrotechnics (white smoke and spark effects). The end result is a matte that can be composited with other elements.

Spill — When the subject stands too close to the green or blue screen, light can reflect off of it and "spill" onto actors or objects, causing keying problems. Parts of the subject will disappear, along with the green screen. Check out the green spill on our actor's shoulder in image 9.7 (color insert).

Background plate — The background image that is composited behind the CG elements or green / blue screen keyed images. This background plate

9.6. The matte created after the keying process.

9.8. The background plate shot on location.

can be filmed on location, or be a CG environment or still image. Most of the time, if the camera is moving, the background plate will also have to move to match the foreground action. Therefore, background plates are normally of a higher resolution or size in order to be able to move around the composite. Background plates are usually shot first so that the lighting on any foreground elements (such as your green screen actors) can match it.

Matte painting — Matte paintings once referred to images painted on sheets of glass to extend a set or create some fantastical part of a movie world. They were painted on glass so they didn't move or sway when filmed and ruin the illusion. Parts of the painting were left clear so that other elements or shots of actors could then be inserted into the space. Today we have digital matte paintings, stitched together from a series of high-resolution stills or CG-rendered images and sometimes used as background plates.

Rotoscoping — The process of manually cutting out your subject from the background image frame by frame to end up with the actor/object isolated as a single element, as if they have been keyed out from a green or blue screen. Rotoscoping is an alternative to creating a matte with a green screen. This is a time-consuming process since the actor or object has to be removed or "cut out" from the frame by hand over the course of the shot, one frame at a time, at 24 (25 in

PAL countries) frames per second. The process of rotoscoping uses a mask to draw around the area in question. Rotoscoping is sometimes favored over keying (if your background plate is also the actual background shot on location) since the lighting of your actor and background will match exactly, being the same shot; conversely, green screen necessitates you match the background lighting in a studio weeks later. Objects or

9.9. A matte painting created in Photoshop.

9.10. Rotoscoping in action to separate elements.

9.11. Smoke and fire elements on a transparent background.

elements such as atmospheres, torna-does, monsters, or explosions can then be placed behind the actor and in front of the background. You may even rotoscope your actor out of the shot and place them in an entirely different environment. The choices are endless. Rotoscoping is also sometimes used as a last resort, with the subject of the shot removed by poorly filmed green screen. Hair or similarly flimsy objects are difficult to rotoscope, as are leaves or plants, which lack a consis-tent shape. Rotoscoping can also be your get-out-of-jail card if there isn't adequate time or resources for a green screen setup on shooting day.

Elements — Elements are smaller parts of a shot that could either be produced using CG from a 3D anima-tion program or shot as live that are placed on top of or under the live-action layers. The elements might be particles of dust, smoke, debris, water, rain, snow, or fire. They could be moving or still-based, and are added to the composition to enhance the story and the reality of the shot. In the image above you can see fire and smoke elements on a trans-parent layer, ready to be placed into a composition. A "particle system" is section of a 3D animation package or standalone program that can generate and animate hundreds or thousands of particles or objects. Any natural forces can then be applied with the computer, such as wind or gravity to create a natural or magical phenom-enon. Particle systems can be used to create falling leaves, snow, rain, smoke, dust, clouds, water, tornadoes, fireworks, or even magic dust.

162

Tracking markers — Tracking markers are colored balls, colored tape, or stickers placed on a green / blue screen when the camera is moving to allow this activity to be "tracked." That movement information (stored as X, Y, and Z coordinates in 3D space) can then be applied to the imported background plate so it can move with the foreground camera shot, suggesting that everything was filmed at the same time.

If you're shooting something as a live-action plate to add CG elements in to, there won't be any green screen tracking markers, instead the compositing software can use markers in the scene itself to help track the shot. Corners of buildings or lampposts can be tracked to get an idea of what the camera is doing. So if you find yourself shooting a moving background plate, make sure you have something in shot that can be tracked that stays in the frame for the entire length of the shot, never getting obscured by anything in the foreground.

Plug-ins — A plug-in is a smaller computer program used in combination with a compositing package or 3D program. Plug-ins cannot run on their own, but must be used within another effects package. Plug-in programs can produce many unique elements, such as particles like smoke and sparks; they also emulate film emulsions, create lens flares, and render many other smaller effects to apply to your shots. Each layer or element within your composited shot might contain many plug-in effects from external programs or the main program itself.

9.12. A tracking marker used to track the cameras movements.

Pre-vis — A moving storyboard. Pre-vis shots can be produced within the same 3D animation package used for the main animation. It's a crude, blocky version of the shots to show other crew members and actors what the shot currently being filmed will look like (and its timings). They can then go to the editor to roughly assemble the film and give a sense of the required timings.

Render — When the compositing or 3D program outputs the final image containing all the elements in their finished and finessed state, it is called a "render." So if you hear of a "render time" being high, you know that a shot is complicated and using extensive processing power. It is then saved in a format and codec that your NLE system can recognize, and is placed back into the edit timeline. A render from a 3D program can be saved as a complete file or executed as various lighting "passes" pieced together within the compositing program. An artist producing a 3D object could render a "diffusion pass," a "specular pass," a "reflection pass," or an "ambient occlusion pass" of that object. All of these lighting variables can be tweaked and adjusted within the final composite, which is then itself rendered out. The big visual effects houses have "render farms": rooms full of interconnected computers maximizing their collective processing power.

To help understand the compositing process, see image 9.13 (color insert) to see a completed breakdown of a visual effects shot.

When you're working with new technology or a new process, no doubt you'll find yourself a little out of your comfort zone. *This is the best way to learn.* You might not pull it off, it might look fake, or you might end up scrapping it altogether, but at least you'll learn. Visual effects work is very time consuming, and your patience will be tested. But when it works, it's a great feeling and could give your blockbuster an epic sense of scale.

COMPOSITING

As mentioned above, a "composite" is when you put all your various elements together and output them to create your shot. You might mix your green screen actor with some CG background smoke and flying CG helicopters, all backdropped by a cityscape image. It's either placing CG elements into live-action background shots or placing live action into CG background shots. Once you have keyed your green screen, adjusted the opacity of the smoke elements, and timed the helicopter flyover, you can render out your final image to be used in your edit timeline. A compositing program is the backbone of any visual effects work. Most of the other programs

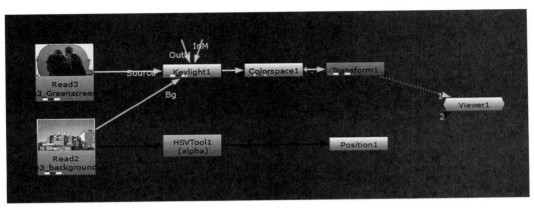

9.14. Node-based compositing.

involved in preparing a visual effects shot will work with, or be producing elements for, the compositing program. Compositing programs have a host of tools at their disposal; they give you the ability to draw masks, color-correct images, add titles, animate images, and track the movements of people or objects in the frame. We as an audience know when something doesn't look right. To properly sell the shot, shadows can be darkened here, or the contrast between the layered elements adjusted.

DIFFERENT TYPES OF COMPOSITING PROGRAMS

To break things down even further, there are two different types of compositing programs. You can either work in "Node" or "Layer" based programs. They do basically the same thing, but approach the task in different ways.

Node — Node compositing shows the source input to final shot output in progression, represented as a tree graph or "node tree," which resembles a flow chart. Node-based compositing is good for a larger composite since its layout makes it easier to keep track of everything, and the order effects are applied is obvious in your workflow. A "node" basically changes a signal. If you had a video signal entering a node that contains color, transparency, and shape values, for example, the node would change those values, altering the outputted file / image to your specifications. The order of when things happen to certain clips is shown by the arrows or "noodles" connecting the nodes.

Layer — Layer-based compositing represents each element or media as a separate layer within a timeline setting, similar to your editing package. Each layer has a time setting for its in and out points and any effects that have

9.15. Layer based compositing

been added. All layers are stacked on top of one another; and if some of the top layers have masks / areas that are transparent, then the layers underneath, like the background plate, can become visible.

USING MASKS IN COMPOSITING

A mask is part of your compositing software that can be used for a few reasons. A mask is a series of lines with connecting points that is hand-drawn over an image to form a complete shape. A mask can extract, like with rotoscoping, or just isolate a chosen area. Maybe you want to remove an unwanted section of the image, or highlight it to apply a color correction or effect. A mask also enables a matte to be generated around a

particular person or object that can later be animated. This, essentially, is rotoscoping. A mask applied to an element or layer gives a transparency value to that element too. A mask can be used to change the shape of something or to cut unwanted items out of frame. Masks are very commonly used in compositing programs to alter the look and shape of things. In the picture below, the image on the left sees a mask applied to the foreground to replace the sky, as seen in the final image on the right.

3D MODELING AND ANIMATION PROGRAMS

Some visual effect shots might require a 3D model. This can be anything from a new or existing building, a

9.16. Before-and-after image sees the actors rotoscoped via masks in order to replace the sky.

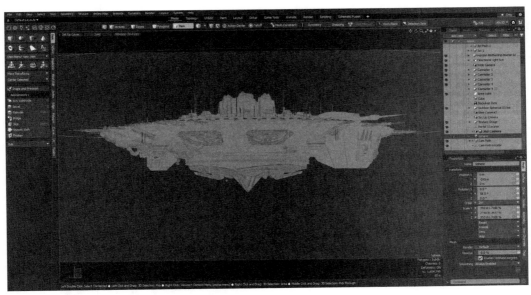

9.17. A 3D model being built within a 3D animation package.

car, spaceship, dinosaur, monster, or digital actors. A 3D model is created within the animation software, textured or "clothed" with materials, animated (if required), and lit to match the live-action environment in which it's to be seen. A virtual camera is also created within the 3D package with the same lens and aperture used to shoot the background plate. This way the model, when framed through this virtual camera, should match the perspective in the live-action element. Once the model is finished, it is rendered out to the file format and resolution required for its compositing, along with any other needed elements. No matter what software you use to create and animate your model, the principles of modeling and animation are the same.

PREPARING FOR A SHOOT INVOLVING VISUAL EFFECTS WORK

A visual effects supervisor, who will be overseeing all the visual effects work in the post-production stage, should be present on the set when you film. They need to make sure that the green screen is lit well, and that tracking markers are present throughout the shot to help the computer match any camera movements. They ensure that they or their team get all the right elements to make up the shot, and that they are all shot correctly. They know to record important camera information for later reference arranging shots: camera height, lens size, camera angle (if it's tilting), aperture, and correct database labeling. If a 3D camera needs to be created in the software program to match the live-action elements, then this information is vital. A camera with these same settings can be created in 3D space to film the animation so it matches the live-action photography, ensuring everything composites together seamlessly.

Storyboards are a must to make sure you and everyone else knows what the shots will look like. This helps the camera operator, the actors, and any other members of the crew know what is trying to be achieved. If you have the time, use a pre-vis animated storyboard to demonstrate movement or how a 3D object might look.

It's fun coming up with the shots and then reverse-engineering how to put them together and integrate them. The director and visual effects super-visor will reverse-engineer and analyze the final shot's appearance, and its preparatory logistics. Like any role, preparation is essential. Each finished shot might have between two and over 100 different elements or layers. It all starts with what you want to see, what angle the shot is, how wide or close the camera is, and what action is transpiring. Visual effects people might get frustrated if you change plans during compositing. Things can be tweaked, of course, and they do change over time. But when big changes are suggested and elements

weren't shot for that purpose, things can become costly.

VISUAL EFFECTS TOOLS ON SET

Visual effects supervisors sometimes use a chrome and gray ball on set, and photograph these objects in the same lighting environment as the scene being filmed.

9.18. Chrome and gray balls — visual effects tools on set.

The chrome ball tells us where the light sources are. It reflects anything bright and gives a position of where the light is coming from. Once you align your lights within the CG envi-ronment, the gray ball imparts how to balance the intensity of your light and how to match levels within the computer. Using these tools allows artists lighting any 3D object or character to match the light from the set and position the 3D model in the frame as seamlessly as possible.

A BREAKDOWN OF A VISUAL EFFECTS SHOT

Take a look at this breakdown of a completed visual effects shot. Here we see a car mirror reflecting the road, and an alien ship in the distance. This shot was made up of five layers of elements to give the illusion of it happening live. At first glance it might seem that the only visual effect is the spaceship, but it required a little more than that. Being shot on the driver's side (in the U.K.) of the car meant that it couldn't be filmed live for practical and safety reasons, so a static image of the mirror was used (as seen in picture 1). A mask was applied, and the mirror was cut from the background to help dispose of the static road behind it (as seen in picture 2). A reverse angle looking out of the back window to show the mirror's reflection was also shot (as seen in picture 3). A CG spaceship was designed and rendered (as seen in picture 4). After the reflecting shot had been added (as seen in picture 5), CG dirt and dust was applied to the mirror to suggest debris on the glass, just like a real wing mirror. From the backseat of the same side of the car, a shot of the road racing by was filmed to be placed behind the mirror (as seen in picture 6). The shot of the reverse reflected image was then tracked for its movement before applying that information to the CG spaceship to move it in time with everything else. This then formed the completed composite (as seen in picture 7).

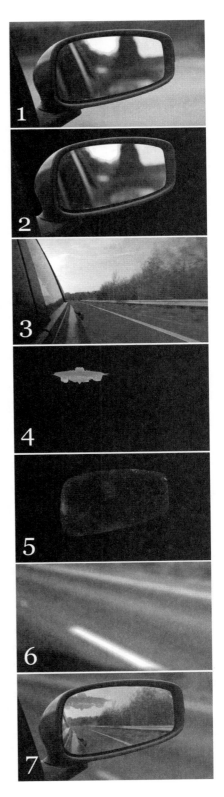

9.19. A complete breakdown of a visual effects shot.

APPROACH

When planning any visual effect shot, consider how the scene would be shot if done practically. If a camera operator was filming this CG scene live, how would they do it? Would the camera be moving? Would your documentary style mean you'd shoot with some crash zooms? What would the camera position be? Would it be ground level looking up, or from the sky? Films like *Jurassic Park* (1993) successfully tried a ground-level approach. All of the dinosaurs were filmed from the characters' point of view. This added a subliminal sense of realism to the CGI, so it played as if it had been filmed for real. *King Kong* (2005) took a slightly different approach: the camera flies all over the environment. This might remind viewers that what they're watching isn't real, since executing those shots practically is very difficult. Are your beautiful visual effects stopping the audience from being completely sucked into your world and fully enjoying the film? Maybe. But just because you can do something doesn't mean you should. Or perhaps *Jurassic Park*'s Ian Malcolm (Jeff Goldblum) said it best: "You're so preoccupied with whether or not you could that you didn't stop to think if you should." Or in keeping with the Spielberg theme, consider his belief that: "If *Jaws* never existed, except in the year 2005, I would have had the digital tools to have had much more

of the shark in the movie. Therefore, I would have ruined much more of the movie!"

Always take your cues for your visual effect shots from the project or the scene at hand, and you can incorporate these stylistic elements into your photography to help sell the shots. On my previous projects, the scene in question might have been photographed documentary style and handheld, so I shot the background plates to match that. However, while on location I've also filmed another take of the same shot locked off on a tripod to give my artist options later in post. Camera shake can always be added to a static shot if need be.

In addition, ask, "Could this shot be achieved practically with a real camera?" As soon as the camera does amazing things, flying here, there, and everywhere, the audience knows they're watching something fake. If it's impossible to do practically, then reconsider your CG camera move. It's the same with any digital characters and stunt work. If a stunt person couldn't do it, then the CG digital stunt person shouldn't either. (Unless they're a superhero, of course.)

Many years incorporating CG elements into shots has revealed that it's not just the CG element itself making a shot look real, but how it interacts with its environment. Its presence might kick up a little dust, cast a shadow over a nearby building, or obscure or be obscured behind an object or person. Optimal shot design involves placing any CG objects behind other objects in the scene to give a sense of depth and realism. Layers and layers of these small elements — smoke, dust, haze, or people — can be added to sell that final shot. Shadows may well make your composition even more believable. Shadows from your 3D animation — dinosaur, spaceship, fighter jet, building — will be cast onto your surroundings. Shadows provide a nice interaction between the CG element and the live-action plate, which binds the two together, giving the impression it was all shot for real on location.

The really big secret to selling visual effect shots: *Try and remove the perfection from the images.* CG shots can look fake because they're manufactured in a computer and not filmed by humans. When we film something live, cameras shake, images overexpose, the focus goes soft before going sharp again, and dirt gets on the lens. Restoring these small aspects to your composite dilutes the perfection and adds a layer of reality to your CG shots.

SHOOTING AND LIGHTING FOR GREEN SCREEN WORK

Using a green screen for film work is very common now, and has a wide range of applications. Green screens come in all shapes and sizes, from a full curtain and floor studio setup to a 3' x 5' foldaway-material version small enough to carry. It all depends on what your shot is and what you're trying to achieve.

When shooting any visual effects involving green screen and keying footage, demand the highest-quality color information from your recorded images. The minimum requirement for high-quality green screen work is a codec with a color sampling of 4:2:2 to execute a good, clean key of the image. Keying requires quality color information in the image, and your camera choice should reflect this.

Identifying the background image enables the director of photography to light the subject in the same way as the background, ensuring the two elements will match perfectly once composited. If the background plate has a low setting sun in the bottom right corner, then that orange glow should appear on the left shoulder of your actor if they're facing the camera. Small touches sell the shot to the audience. Position your actor far enough from the green screen to avoid any spill from the screen itself. If too close to the screen, the green color can reflect or spill onto the actor, and when you remove the green screen, you'll also remove part of them. Being too close to the screen also means that when you light the actor, they might cast shadows back onto the green screen. These issues alone sometimes mean you'll need a bigger screen than you think. And you must always ensure the actor's movements stay within the scope of the green screen. If they wave their arms even for a second, and their fingertips go outside of the green screen (but still in shot), you'll lose them. (You would mask or roto-scope around their hands to salvage the shot if this happened.)

The green screen needs to be lit separately from the actor, and also evenly lit across the breadth of the screen if the actor is moving in front of these areas. Having it darker at one end will result in varying strengths of green, making keying the shot harder for the visual effects artist. The screen around the actor should be even, with no creases or folds. The software will remove the green color, but any obvious texture in the material will transfer to your background image. Imagine you painted a wall of bricks green and used them as your green screen. Once keyed, the green would disappear, but the brick texture would then be applied to your background plate.

The angle at which you film your actor, and your camera height, tilt angle, and lens size, must all match the background plate you are using. It must look like the composited shot was all filmed at the same time.

Having a different lens size or height will destroy this illusion.

Some DPs like to expose the green screen one f-stop over the one being used to shoot the actor. Having that extra brightness and solid green means the edges of the actor can be easily defined. Others light it to the same stop, and some a stop under. If the green screen is too bright, you can lose saturation, and there is a little danger of more spill on the actor. Everyone has their own preferred method. Personally, I think lighting a stop over is good. The problems arise when you go too far in either direction — too bright or too dark. I've sat in a visual effects suite where the screen was too dark to pull a good key. Also talk with whoever is in charge of costuming so that the actor isn't wearing anything green — it could result in that part of the actor also disappearing from the shot! Although current software is sophisticated, and keying programs can differentiate between different shades and color saturations of green, this scenario is still best avoided. Failing that, try a bluescreen instead. However, if you are filming a scene with a floating head, or maybe a war film with a character missing an arm, wrapping their arm or body in blue or green material could give you the means of achieving this shot.

If the camera is locked off, then no tracking markers will be required.

However, if you pan, tilt, or do any type of camera movement during the shot, then you'll need markers to track and record the camera's new position. The compositing software can then apply those new movement coordinates to the background image.

As mentioned, keying software is very intuitive now and can make allowances for poor green screen work. Sometimes the shoot is rushed, or the resources just aren't there to do the best job you can. You might well have an uneven green screen containing the odd fold, but software can now somewhat compensate for this. Within the keying application there are various parameters and variables that can be adjusted to pull a solid key. Of course, this shouldn't result in a carefree, "Oh, it will be fine . . ." attitude on set, but

if you are down to the wire, there are ways to fix things in the application. Having an even green screen only applies to the areas around the subject, though. There is no issue if the sides of the green screen are uneven and the light levels fall off, but the actor isn't moving near that area. A "garbage matte" to mask off the uneven area can easily be produced. It's fine if the actor is perfectly lit and so is the green screen, but the shot is wider than the green screen and also captures some of the set, ceiling, or surrounding area. When the artist pulls a key from the shot, they can mask around the unwanted elements and create the garbage matte. Then the software can be told to pull the key and remove the green from what is within the garbage-matte mask, as in the picture below:

9.20. Filming wider than the green screen is achievable if garbage mattes are used.

The secret to any visual effects work is preplanning. Do this before you get to the studio or location. Ask questions like: *What is the action? How wide are we?* I've seen directors ask for walking shots in front of green screens only big enough to shoot a medium from the waist up. A green screen does not, unfortunately, mean you can shoot anything. Planning and preparation are again crucial here.

RESOURCES

You might find yourself needing to use some pyrotechnics or pyrotechnic elements in your epic action-filled blockbuster. There are a few ways of achieving this: You could use live on-set pyro, which we looked at in the special effects section; you could film live pyro against a black screen and key out the black to digitally composite the elements; you can create your own digital pyro using a plug-in program designed for that purpose; or you can utilize a number of packages now available selling pre-keyed practical effects that you can composite yourself.

Many online companies now sell 2K / 4K resolution live action or digital elements. It could be large smoke plumes, ricochets, fire, explosions, sparks, debris, or water. It still takes skill and finesse to use these layers subtly and make the shot real and believable, but doing so saves the artists and filmmakers a tremendous amount of time. Filming

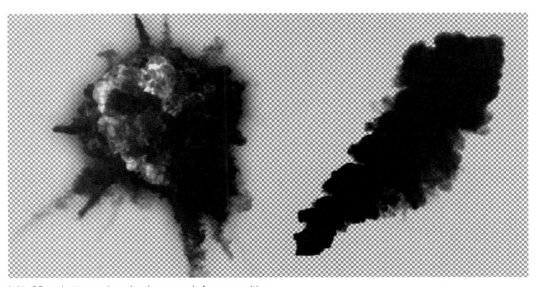

9.21. CG explosions and smoke plumes ready for compositing.

backgrounds and then compositing these elements also allows you to correctly time events that might be left to the gods if done live. To make these CG elements look realistic and believable, don't just focus on the main CG explosion or element itself. Incorporate other elements around it to help reflect how it interacts with its environment. Look closely at the debris and smoke and how they light up their surroundings by adding glows to nearby buildings on the background plate. Create a sense of depth to the shot by adding a layer of foreground action atop the CG element, partially obscuring it. This could be a car hood, a person, a wall, or a street sign. This added depth helps make the explosion or CG element look real by placing it more securely in its surroundings.

WEAPONS AND VISUAL EFFECTS

Firing blanks on set can be very loud and dangerous. BB or airsoft replica weapons offer a quieter and slightly safer alternative utilizing visual effects instead. Adding shells and muzzle flashes to your shots is now even easier with online visual effect companies offering pre-keyed packages featuring a host of various elements.

I've found the best replica weapons are airsoft guns; they look the most realistic. Use ones with a blowback recoil function, one where the slide (the top section of the gun) jolts back and forth to show that the gun has been fired. Your visual effects artist is then able to add digital muzzle flash and a shell casing ejecting. Making the shell casing look as realistic as possible requires fast-moving animation and

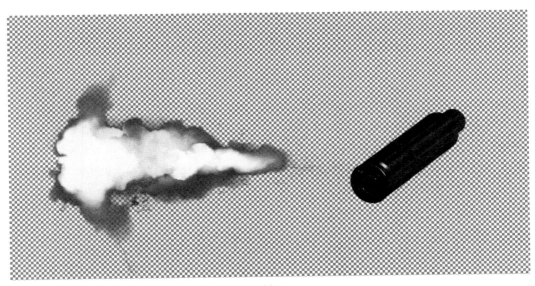

9.22. CG muzzle flashes and shell casings ready for compositing.

9.23. A CG muzzle flash in action.

added blur. It's not necessary to seek perfection from CG elements or images. If you really were firing a gun or even shooting blanks, your eye wouldn't be able to see each and every shell clearly for its entire journey from barrel ejection port to floor. Configure the animated CG shell layer so you can only just glimpse it, maybe only seeing every other one. *You may not able to see them all clearly, but you'd miss them if they were gone.* It's when the artist wants their work to be seen that things begin to look fake. Take a look at the image above to see muzzle flashes and shell casings in action.

FINALLY, A NOTE ABOUT ACTORS

Any visual effect is only as good as the actor's performance reacting to it. If the reaction is flat and uninspired, then the awesome visual effect will be lessened. Sometimes, lesser-trained or beginning actors might feel inhibited acting their heart out or crying to a tennis ball eyeline marker before the cute CG creature has been added. It is up to you, the director, to make them feel secure and trust that what they are doing on set will look amazing once the CG elements are added later on.

CHAPTER 10

MUSIC IN YOUR BLOCKBUSTER

"Music is dialogue."
— RIDLEY SCOTT, DIRECTOR

Like most filmmaking tools today, music has become more widely available to new filmmakers through the advent of better technology and compositional tools on the internet. Just like visual effects, the tools, hardware, and software are now readily available for up-and-coming composers to try their hand at being the new John Williams or Hans Zimmer. Gone are the days of needing access to a full orchestra.

When working with music and composers, the music is there to support the film. Always. It's never the other way around. It is never there for the sake of the music. If it were, you'd be at a concert, not the theater. The same applies to the sound mix, too.

We're not going to discuss musical composition here, but it is worth looking at how and when to use music, as well as the process of working with a composer. I've had the pleasure of working with several composers and learning their approaches and methods.

MY EXPERIENCES

To include music in my earliest films, I played songs on tape — live as my friends and I shot! When the shot finished, someone pressed "pause" on the portable stereo. The music may have sounded a little choppy, but it worked for our purposes. When you're 11, it's cool just to make a movie. Eventually, when I got my hands on a small five-channel audio mixer, I mixed scores from our favorite blockbusters over our in-camera-edited films.

My early work ignited my thought processes and opinions regarding when to begin and when to end the music in my films. Finally, when contacts and budgets grew, I started working with real composers. Hearing a new piece of music composed just for your film really gets the heart racing; you begin to see everything come together. My experiences with these talented crewmembers have on the whole been very positive, but having a difference of opinion with someone certainly tests your diplomatic skills. Music can take a very long time to compose. There's thinking and planning: the musicians must learn their parts, and the recordings must be mixed, layered, and balanced. Changing elements can take a lot of time and effort, and it ups the cost. Talk at length with your composer, and really let them know what you're after by including a temp score over the rough edit. Talk is cheap; remixing isn't.

SPOTTING

"Spotting" is the process whereby composer and director sit down with the locked edit of the film to establish where music should feature. Any particular story beats that need to be cued or enhanced will be discussed. A musical cue signifies to the audience that this moment is important, or that the film wants you to feel something. You're spotting for emotion, cueing that emotional beat. Placement of film music is all about peaks and valleys. If you have a particular moment you'd like to emphasize with music, and there already is music playing from earlier in the film, you might diminish the impact of the point you want punctuated. Perhaps you don't score the moments leading up to that important part to maximize its desired impact. The presence of music is just as powerful as the absence of it. Let's look at a few examples. The first is the score for Michael Mann's film *Heat* (1995) by Elliot Goldenthal. The film tells the story of a group of bank robbers led by Robert De Niro who are being hunted by the LA Police Department, headed by Al Pacino. The film features a large-scale shootout in the streets of downtown LA after a robbery. During the robbery, Goldenthal scores the suspense, and a ticking clock beat keeps us on edge as the robbers raid the bank vault. The cops are gathering outside, and the scene is set for the biggest exchange of gunfire ever put to film. However, just as the tension mounts and the robbers exit the bank to see the waiting cops, the music comes to a halt. Then the sound effects take over; gunfire, ricochets, and bullet hits come to the forefront of the sound mix. This adds a layer of realism that likely surpasses the effect of a score just getting louder or more intense.

The other example is Alan Silvestri's score for Robert Zemeckis's film *Cast Away* (2000). The film tells the story of Chuck Noland (Tom Hanks), who after a plane crash gets stranded on a desert island for four years. It was an interesting and creative choice for composer Alan Silvestri not to score the film until 1 hour 33 minutes in. That means no music over the opening titles, no music to enhance the plane crash, and most importantly, no music to show how lonely and sad it was for Hanks's character. The opportunity to really make the audience feel sad for Chuck was dismissed, as music or any pleasant sound would in an abstract kind of way, comfort him. This was a daring decision, but no doubt the right one. When Hanks's character finally escapes the island, he turns to see the place that he has called home for the past four years; the score comes in and really hits the emotional beat. A brave choice on the part of the composer and the director. *Cast Away* director Robert Zemeckis: *"Ask: What is the emotional undercurrent that the music is playing? And if there's not an answer for that, then there shouldn't be any music."*

If you're spotting for emotion, you have to make sure that the music reflects the level of emotion on screen. Bringing in the strings too soon and prematurely telling the audience that they are supposed to feel sadness or joy risks losing them by making them feel manipulated. There is nothing wrong with sentiment. Sentiment is good, but go too far and you're at risk of dipping into mawkishness.

Finally, in the film *Mission: Impossible* (1996), Tom Cruise's Ethan Hunt must break into a top-secret room in the CIA building. This

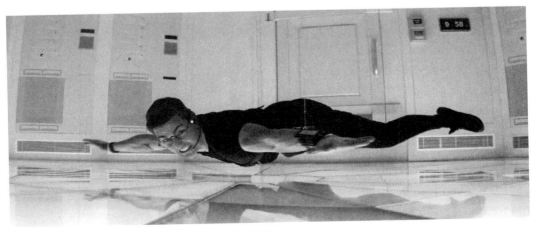

10.1. Tom Cruise as Ethan Hunt in *Mission: Impossible* (1996).

scene is all about sound. A host of security precautions are in place when the room is locked. If the noise level goes above a certain decibel, an alarm is triggered. Every nuance of sound is front and center; the risk of detection is omnipresent. Composer Danny Elfman sensibly leaves the scene devoid of music. To score this scene would remove the tension. The audience is hanging on to every little sound and pin drop, and they simply wouldn't be able to if the sound were muffled or drowned out by music.

LOCKED EDITS

As composing music can be very time-consuming and costly, make sure the version of the film the composer is working with is a locked edit. If it's not, and some changes might be made later in post-production, the composer must be fully briefed before tackling the rough edit. You might send your composer the rough cut just so they can get a feel for where the film is going and what they might write. Do not send your composer the final cut until the edit is locked. Some musical scores might be dependent on frame-accurate edits; the beat in the music times with some big moment on screen. Adding or taking away shots (or even frames) from a scene before a cue will cause that cue to be out of time.

I send the composer a low-res MP4 file of the whole film with a timecode burnt in onscreen. The file is low-res so that their composing software can load the file and play it back at the correct speed without any lags or jumps because of computer memory power. When finished, the composer can then send me the final music tracks as high-quality WAV or AIFF sound file extensions to be placed back into the edit timeline or final mix. They attach a note to tell me the exact timecodes where the various tracks should start.

TEMP SCORES

Sometimes a temp score is placed over a film during the edit. It can be a previous score by the composer, or music taken from an existing film soundtrack. Some composers like hearing a temp score, and some don't. They are helpful to an editor or director evaluating a scene, and also to a composer seeking more informa-tion about a director's vision. The composer might have a completely different take on a scene, and you should be open and welcome their input. If you don't talk the musical language used by a composer, having a temp score helps focus your thoughts and give you a creative foundation. A director speaks of emotion with the composer. What do you want the audience to feel? Let the composer translate that. Hollywood releases often use temp scores throughout post-production and in early screenings. The actual score is most likely the last element completed, so a temp score can prove very useful.

TONE

You might not be able to discuss music composition with your composer, but what you *can* talk to the composer about is tone. Tone is an element each director must learn to control; otherwise, the emotion of a film can shift all over the place. Tone helps answer 99% of the questions raised by crew members before or during the shoot. If a scene has your hero escaping the villains accompanied by dramatic music, the audience will conclude he's in danger and facing serious consequences. If, however, some light-hearted, comedic music was to play over the chase, the audience would know that the hero isn't concerned by the apparent threat, and they will most likely escape this situation unharmed. A great example of this is the finale to the action comedy *Beverly Hills Cop III* (1994). All three lead characters have been shot multiple times during the end gun battle. Once the villain has been dispersed and the character's hobble

together, we hear a comedic rendition of the film's theme, perfectly letting the audience know their wounds are not life-threatening. Here's *Die Hard* (1988) director John McTiernan's thoughts on music: "Very often the music will let the audience know it's okay to think this is ridiculous because the storytellers think this is ridiculous." Tone helps let the audience know where they are. Once you have discussed tone, cue placement, and other issues with the composer, they can ascertain what they might bring to your project. I've always been amazed at how a good composer can recognize a tiny moment in a scene and find the perfect instrument to underscore it on screen. It can be a little motif that nods to the audience what might be happening.

Like any good artist, whether they're a composer or any other member of the team, it all comes down to the story you're trying to tell, not a string section you're showing off or a new toy you're using. It all depends what suits the story.

TELLING THE TRUTH

Music, on the whole, should tell the truth. If music is supporting the emotion of the scene, don't mislead or lie to your audience. If you do, they might not forgive or trust you again. John Williams, the composer for

Steven Spielberg's film *Jaws* (1975), heeded this advice when scoring the shark attacks. The famous *Jaws* theme only comes in when there is a real shark attack. If we thought an attack might happen but it turned out to just be kids playing around, there was no score accompanying these hoax attacks. The reasoning behind this approach has value. If someone shouts and alarms us, but is just crying wolf, we might not be inclined to believe them the next time, even if they're for real. If the filmmakers trick the audience into feeling scared when the outcome is nothing, they risk diminishing the threat and the amount viewers can be scared since they've been tricked once before. Your music builds trust with the audience. Sadly, modern horror movies sometimes don't take this approach, using any opportunity to score every last creak in the floorboards and noise from some dark area of the house, even when it turns out to just be the family cat.

Music is a wonderful tool to have in your filmmaking arsenal. A good score can elevate a scene that falls short elsewhere. It can paper over some, but not all, of the cracks in your edit, bailing you out. Music, just like editing, is about manipulating the viewer, and it can point your audience in the direction you want them to go.

10.2. Roy Scheider as Chief Martin Brody in *Jaws* (1975).

CHAPTER 11

SOUND IN YOUR BLOCKBUSTER

"The only way to deal with chaotic battles is to figure out what to lose. 'Cause at the end of the day, if I played everything I had, it would be sonic mud."

— CHRIS BOYES, RERECORDING MIXER ON *RETURN OF THE KING*

EASY TO ADD, NOT TO TAKE AWAY

Before we look at post sound, let's consider a few approaches when on set. During shooting, you want to record usable sound elements: clean dialogue, and wild tracks (recordings of the ambient sound in the filming area) without anyone moving or talking. You can assemble all those components during the sound mix. It's easier to add things than to take away. On set, look out for actors eating, banging plates and cups, or performing an action while talking. These sounds might "bang" and "clang" over dialogue making it hard to hear the lines, so rubber mats stuck underneath objects muffle noise that might interfere with dialogue

being heard. Directors might want it "real," with all overlapping sound; that is certainly possible, but it's best to make your audio sound real in the mix, not on the day of shooting. Once in the sound mix, you can adjust the level of that clanging to your heart's content. Some sound recordists also like to put carpet on the ground to deaden footsteps. Footsteps can be added later, but if they are recorded on set on the same audio channel as dialogue, you may have trouble independently adjusting their volume. Since clean sound is utterly irrelevant if we don't get all the shots, do spend time recording clean dialogue, but not at the expense of the coverage. You need to use common sense on the day; if the actor's footsteps are audible, but not loud enough to interfere with dialogue, record the scene as presented. The audience can see they are walking, and anticipate hearing the appropriate sounds. If you lose too much time trying to eliminate every other sound, the recordist may go home happy with his or her work, but not the director or editor. There wasn't time to get the shots that could make it all come together and properly tell the story.

ELEMENTS OF POST SOUND

Let's look at the elements of post-production sound that your blockbuster will undoubtedly feature.

Track laying — This is the process of layering all your sound elements and making them ready for the final mix. Each element is given its own audio track so it can be clearly seen and adjusted. What elements do we need to think about when mixing our film? First up is the all-important . . .

Dialogue — This is everything that is said, mumbled, shouted, or whispered that was recorded as production sound on set. The human story is the most important, and therefore dialogue is king. If we can't understand what someone is saying, we are at risk of being taken out of the story. The whole film could rest on one line; if

that line is unclear, you're in trouble. If it is unclear or you want to change the inflection or delivery of a line after you have filmed the scene, you are into the area of ADR (Automated Dialogue Replacement), also called "looping."

ADR — You record ADR with your cast members in a studio weeks or months after the scene has been shot. Maybe you filmed next to an airport runway and the production sound recordist was only able to record a guide track, in which case the line / scene would be ADR'd or revoiced. If you're on a budget, and you won't have access to a recording studio during post, find a quiet place near the location and record the line quite soon after the actor has performed the original scene. This way they won't need to remember how they felt or how they delivered the line all those months ago, as it will still be fresh in their mind. ADR is a lot of work. The quality of the recording will be different, the ambient sound surrounding the actor's line will have to be added, and the line will no doubt have to be finessed to match the surrounding bass and tone frequencies. Try to use the same microphone — ideally a shotgun microphone — to record the dialogue for ADR. Consider the position of the microphone in relation to the actor on screen too.

Foley — Foley, named after its creator Jack Foley, is the reproduction of any sounds made from an actor interacting with objects, clothes, or their environment. Leather jackets creaking, objects placed on a table, footsteps on gravel, heavy chain armor rubbing — basically everything that the character makes happen. Foley is sometimes interpretations of a sound rather than the literal sound itself. Mixers like to add drama and emotion that the real sound would not convey if recorded on its own. Maybe you want a sound for your zombie having its arm ripped off? You could crack open a watermelon or head of lettuce and rip it apart. A punch to the body? Try a rolled-up newspaper being hit with a soft wooden stick . . .

Effects tracks — The effects track comprises any sounds that weren't recorded on location or need to be enhanced. Gunshots, glass shattering, car horns, sirens, alarms . . . These are added later, during post-production; you don't want too many sounds recorded on location (apart from dialogue). Mixing too many sounds could make for a very muddled edit. However, on low-budget films some of the production sound could be used in the mix since there might not be the time or money to add everything later. You need these effects on a separate track in order to control their volume at any given moment. You might record your own sound effect, or use one of the many effects libraries and websites offering downloads, sometimes for free.

Atmos / background ambience — If the sound recordist has done their job well, any background noise from the location will be minimal and only the dialogue will have been recorded. Therefore any ambient sounds are often added in post to give the scene a layer of reality and make the setting feel real. It could be general room tone, wind, singing birds, or gentle crowd ambience. Even if there is silence, there will often be a quiet layer of sound of some kind. Wind, creaky space, and distant voices all tell you there is no sound in the current room, giving the impression of silence. *It is never actual silence.* Atmosphere tracks can be used to create drama, or a feeling of loneliness, or a vast expanse outside. On set, a sound recordist can record a wild track, which consists of a 1–2 minute recording of the ambient sound in the location. A good room tone or wild track of the location can save you if you discover sound gaps between words while editing dialogue.

Music — The musical score often forms an important part of the sound mix. When do we bring up the music, when we do fade it out, and how long might that fade be? Do we go with what the composer has given us, or edit and mix it up a little? Do we

11.1. In the sound-mixing theater.

even need this particular music cue? What music will maximize a scene's emotional weight?

Once the sound designer / dialogue editor (potentially two different people) have done their work, and have amassed all these elements, it's time for the final mix to put them all together. All the elements that have been crafted, added, recorded, and produced are then mixed together at their desired volume levels to create the overall soundscape. Final mixes can take anywhere from one day to three months to complete depending on a film's length and complexity. The mix could also have slight acoustic differences that vary with the viewing platform. If it's for TV, it might have a slightly different mix than if it's for the cinema or online.

If you find you are in a nice high-end studio setting for your final mix, you will be listening to the tracks on very high-quality speakers. You will hear everything you lay down at the right levels. Not everyone will be listening to the soundtrack on equipment of that standard, however (perhaps only at the premiere, through the cinema's high-end speakers). Some mixing studios run the mix through a poor-quality TV speaker to see how it sounds through a normal TV or online. Elements of the mix, like those tiny little nuances of sounds you laid in, could well be missing when played through this normal TV / phone speaker.

MUSIC AND EFFECTS (M&E) MIX

Having all your sound elements on separate tracks is essential if you intend to distribute and sell your movie to foreign territories. Foreign distributors will require what is called an M&E (Music and Effects) mix. Basically, it's everything except dialogue; they will be rerecording this element in the language they are distributing it. This might not be as easy as it sounds; some dialogue tracks recorded during production might also include other sounds that haven't been added in Foley or on a track-lay effects session since they were present on the original dialogue track. When the dialogue is replaced for foreign territories, this sound will now have to be added to the effects track.

PREPARING FOR YOUR POST-PRODUCTION SOUND WORK

If you are the editor of your film as well as the sound designer / mixer, you might well be track-laying and mixing your film all within your editing package.

If you are doing the work yourself, lay all your audio elements out on separate audio tracks on your timeline. For example: Track 1/2 dialogue, person A; 3/4 dialogue, person B; 5/6 sound effects; 7/8 atmosphere & ambience; 9/10 Foley; 11/12 music. Of course, you might end up with many more channels than this if you have more than two people in the scene or multiple channels for atmosphere and effects.

When you prepare dialogue tracks, get in the habit of "checker-boarding" your individual dialogue audio clips. It's called checker-boarding since complete it looks like a chess or checkerboard, as per the diagram below:

11.2. Checker-boarding the various sound tracks in the edit.

By separating the audio clips, you can add very small fades or dissolves to the start and end of one to integrate it with a timeline. It allows a clip to sound smoother without a sudden drop-in of sound, especially if there is a little background noise on the production audio track. This four-frame dissolve, mixed with the atmosphere / ambient wild track underneath, will create smooth-sounding audio. If preparing this work yourself, invest in and use a good pair of headphones. Don't trust your computer speakers or monitor for this task. I did this in my very early work, and upon playback on different equipment heard my audio sharply cutting in and out in a way not audible on my old setup. If you are doing some sound prep work to hand over to the sound mixer, you need to know how to export and deliver your audio files so the audio is right for their system. This is done by exporting what is called an OMF (Open Media Framework) or AAF (Advanced Authoring Format) file. An OMF file saves picture, sound, or both in their full size and quality, and maintains the timing and layout from your edit system. Once the sound mix is complete, the mixer can export a high-quality WAV or similar format as a single file or as multiple sound stems. The sound stems are usually dialogue, effects, and music. You can place them in your edit timeline to replace original sound.

A FEW ADVENTURES IN THE SOUND MIX

One of my favorite parts of post-production, and the filmmaking process as a whole, is the sound mix. Not only is the end of your film in sight, but it is here that you can really see (and hear!) your scenes come to life. It is an opportunity to add to the world that has been created so far. It widens the environment and makes the audience feel that there is so much more going on just outside the frame. It also adds that blockbuster shine, increasing the production value of the piece: a crowd of 30 can become 100, a little disturbance can become chaos, your CG monster can come alive. You help craft the emotional involvement of your audience by dictating what they hear and when. Like any area of production, you do have to keep its elements in check. It's about figuring out what sounds are important and prominent to best tell the story.

I've worked with both experienced sound mixers and some who were just starting out. Some early mixes involve a discussion about what sounds real and what doesn't. Newer sound mixers sometimes think a little too much about a piece and how it reflects reality. Sounds don't necessarily have to be what is real, but what the audience *believes* to be real. Putting a sound effect to everything or precisely mimicking the acoustics of a room might be real and reflect what events actually sound like, but movie sound is different. Some sounds might need to be louder or clearer to best convey important story points, so you can be more selective in what audiences hear. There is no sound in space and very little is audible underwater, but as audiences we expect to hear the spaceships or bubbles or whatever is on screen. In reality we would likely struggle to hear people talking in a nightclub or in the center of a hurricane, but in the movies, all dialogue is magically clear. Two characters walking on the street toward camera from 150 feet away shouldn't be heard by the camera, but they are. If we were looking to reflect reality, we wouldn't hear them clearly until they were maybe five feet away, but in the film world we are allowed to stretch reality. It's not about exactly reflecting the onscreen action, but offering an interpretation of it. That interpretation is the sound designer and sound mixer's work.

Real sounds of a particular object don't always sound correct when matching onscreen action either, and need to be augmented by additional, unrelated sounds. For example, an explosion sound might be made up of a real explosion, a pig squeal, a lion growl, and a cannon being fired. Sound design is all about solid storytelling. It's the presence of sounds in the background you're after, not how noises would *actually* sound.

You don't need to hear every single crash, bang, and wallop that has a corresponding onscreen action, either. Less can be more, or it can be counterintuitive. Sounds cancel each other out; if you hear everything on screen at once, you'll end up with noise. Sometimes in action movies, bullet sounds, whiz-bys, ricochets, and impacts can all get on top of one another, and it can become very messy very quickly. Pick the right sounds at the right time to portray all these things happening at once. Use your sound levels to make more of your desired impact. Explosions and the like can be really loud without cranking the volume up to 11. You can build in beats of near silence by sucking out all the surrounding sound *just before* your big explosion; it now *appears* the sound was louder. This way it sounds dynamic and has the impact you're after without distorting your soundtrack. Once a sound like pouring rain has been established, it can readily be pushed to the back of the mix with a slightly lower volume when characters start talking. The audience can still hear the rain, but it doesn't need to be at the volume it was when you first introduced it.

The work in the mix is invisible if it's done right. You are looking to get the film to a high technical standpoint with the correct levels and balances and so on, but the real work comes in your creative choice of sounds, knowing when to bring them in or fade them out, or cut them from the mix altogether.

CONCLUSION

*"What does the audience want? Well, they don't know
what they want. They just know that they want it, and
they'll know what that is when they see it."*

— CHRISTOPHER NOLAN, WRITER / DIRECTOR

So as we come to a close, I want to move away from the hands-on creative stuff and talk about a few other areas I've encountered during my filmmaking endeavors; I have found these to be the secrets to making, and more importantly completing, your blockbuster.

Here's the first: *Work to a higher standard.* Whatever area you're working in — writing, lighting, directing, editing, visual effects, music, or sound mixing — ask: *Can this be better?* Is the script good enough? Can you live with those overexposed areas of the frame? Can this scene be cut tighter and more effectively? So many people in so many fields are satisfied with just average. What are

you prepared to sacrifice to get your project where it needs to be? Time, leisure, money, travel, sleep? How amazing will your film be if every area gets elevated from very good to excellent to outstanding? Obviously, filmmaking is a compromise, but never let your work be of a lower standard because of a rash judgment or a poor attitude.

The second thing is: *passion.* Passion tends to separate those who will be successful and those who won't. This applies to filmmaking, acting, writing, or any discipline within the industry. Passion drives us. Passion is what gets us up early to write, or to drive hundreds of miles to a meeting, or to finesse the edit until 2 am. When things go in a direction you didn't anticipate or get tough, passion is what will carry you through those hard times. Doubt will kick in, you'll receive criticism, you'll be rejected — passion can keep your emotional defenses high. You need to eat, sleep, dream about your film. If you aren't, don't attempt it. Your blockbuster will take over your life for years, going from script to set, from post-production to festivals. You'll need a lot of fuel to keep you going, and that fuel is passion.

The third thing is: *managing the opinion of others*. At each stage of making your film, you will encounter people giving you their opinion. Whether it regards the script, the set dressing, or your editing choices. The questions to ask begin with: Who is this person? And do you value their opinion? The trick is to surround yourself with likeminded people who will give you their honest opinion of your work. They should be filmmakers of sorts — experienced directors and producers who have read scripts and understand the process. No matter what, *make sure they are accomplished and have a trained eye.* You have to be mindful of other people's comments and understand their sensibilities. A writer friend reviewing my work memorably commented, "I wouldn't go in this direction or tell this story myself, but I can see what you're trying to do and will help you along

that road as best I can." This was fantastic! He wasn't trying to turn my script into what he thought it should be, but help me make the thing I was trying to make. Don't be too quick to dismiss feedback or a note if you don't agree with it. It could be that the point behind the note is valid but the way the feedback was presented was misleading. Understand a note's meaning as well as possible, then decide how seriously to consider it.

I have listened to people before on set or in the edit when I shouldn't have, and watched my idea slowly edge away because all those small deviations added up to a substandard final piece. I should have stood my ground more, and have regretted not doing so, so trust your intuition. *If you have to make a mistake, at least make it of your own volition so you can learn from it.* There is nothing worse than watching something that doesn't work because you listened to others' voices and not your own.

Editors I know have purposely left in longer edits or redundant shots just so the producers, executive producers, or whoever can have something to suggest taking out. This way the producers feel that they have contributed to the piece, even though it was suggesting removing things the editor had wanted to change anyway. If the editor submits a solid cut, the parties giving input might still suggest removing shots that will then damage the film. You may agree with this approach or not; it occurs purely so people can feel that they have contributed and earned their position. Of course, producers, executives, and the powers that be do make very good suggestions, and their years of experience do play vital roles. *But sometimes politics demand that people feel involved.* Therefore, respect must be given to the secure viewer who after watching the cut says that they have nothing to add and that the editor shouldn't change a frame.

If you know in the deepest part of your gut that you want to do something a certain way, but others advise against it, you should still do it. You know you are correct in your method and approach and this is your project, not theirs. They have not lived with the script, idea, or film as long and as deeply as you have. History is filled with people who have gone against the grain and made or shot something against what convention has suggested with extraordinary results. That could be you.

The above three concepts are worth mastering. They all play a part when creating something of value, whether making films, writing, painting, making music, or doing anything of an artistic nature. These ideas and your efforts to use them effectively are crucial to the quality of your work and creative vision.

It's time to get to work! We've covered a lot in this book, but you're up to the challenge. Audiences are ready and waiting for your blockbuster. They want to be entertained, educated, and inspired. Don't let them down. See you at the movies!

SOURCES

INTRODUCTION

"The best advice I could give is to take your work to the imaginative extreme, as far as you can creatively go. Be dangerous. If it has enough of your voice and passion in it, others will see it as original, and it will stand out and get noticed." — Pen Densham, author interview

CHAPTER 1: WRITING YOUR BLOCKBUSTER

Nolan quote on backstory: www.variety.com/2017/film/news/christopher-nolan-dunkirk-oscars-movies-tv-spielberg-1202607836

James Mangold quote on character — taken from the *Logan* "making of" Blu-ray

Jonathan Demme's refrigerator questions: As mentioned in *Screenwriters' Masterclass* by Kevin Conroy Scott

The script of the blockbuster hit *Batman* (1989) called for Jack Nicholson's Joker to drag Vicki Vale (Kim Basinger) to the top of the cathedral in Gotham City in the finale of the film. On set, Nicholson asked director Tim Burton, "Why am I walking up these stairs? Where am I going?" and Burton replied, "We'll talk about it when you get to the top." Burton added, "I had to tell him I didn't know . . ." Quoted in Tom Shone, *Blockbuster*

CHAPTER 2: PRODUCING YOUR BLOCKBUSTER

"You have to be a self-starter, initiating every phone call, soliciting every meeting — as many as it takes to get the answer you want or the results you need." — Lawrence Turman, *So You Want to Be a Producer*

The Duellists story on reusing prop urns on set taken from the DVD commentary by Ridley Scott

CHAPTER 3: CASTING YOUR BLOCKBUSTER

"The greatest mistake a young director can make is to want to show the actor what to do. It's like asking an artist to design a poster but sketching it for him. An actor is a *performer*." — Jean-Pierre Jeunet, taken from *Moviemakers' Master Class* by Laurent Tirard

Instead, Spielberg dressed up the boy's make-up artist in a gorilla suit and placed them behind the camera. Later in the scene, the make-up artist removed the gorilla mask so the boy saw it was actually a friendly face underneath messing around, and the child's expression changed accordingly. — James Kendrick, *Darkness in the Bliss-Out: A Reconsideration of the Films of Steven Spielberg*

CHAPTER 4: FILMING YOUR BLOCKBUSTER

"All of one's experience of life subconsciously informs every creative decision one makes. That's what makes each individual cinematographer different." — Janusz Kaminski, ASC (*American Cinematographer* magazine, July 2004, p. 42)

"In 1990, 80 percent of theatrical wide releases in the U.S. were in the 1.85:1 aspect ratio. In 2010, only 29 percent were 1.85:1. In those two decades, there was a clear straight-line decline in 1.85:1 movies and an equal straight-line increase in 2.39:1 movies. In 2016, 71 percent of theatrical releases in the U.S. were 2.39:1, 20 percent were 1.85:1, and 9 percent were 'other' aspect ratios, including 1.78:1 and even the traditional Academy aspect ratio of 1.37:1." (*American Cinematographer* magazine, January 2018, p. 26)

Sydney Pollack on moving the camera on *The Firm* taken from *Moviemakers' Master Class* by Laurent Tirard

CHAPTER 5: DIRECTING YOUR BLOCKBUSTER

"The job of a film director is to tell the story through the juxtaposition of uninflected images." — David Mamet, *On Directing Film*

Renny Harlin one-impressive-shot-a-day approach — as discussed on the *Die Hard 2* DVD commentary

CHAPTER 6: FIREARMS, STUNTS, AND FIGHTS IN YOUR BLOCKBUSTER

"Everybody says CGI is the death of stunt people, but it's not. They still need people to physically perform; otherwise, you turn into a cartoon." — Vic Armstrong, www.kungfukingdom.com/interview-with-vic-armstrong

CHAPTER 7: SPECIAL EFFECTS IN YOUR BLOCKBUSTER

"It's really not about the tool; it's about your imagination and what you bring to the film and the shot. The tool doesn't matter."— Dennis Muren, *Encore!* (www.France24.com); www.youtube.com/watch?v=h052j4Kum_k

CHAPTER 8: EDITING YOUR BLOCKBUSTER

Terry Rawlings editing quote: Interview with *Diegesis* magazine. www.youtube.com/watch?v=2i6YN6A-cLw

"Every film has a turkey shot." — Michael Bay, *Transformers* DVD commentary

"I think it's dangerous to [look at the film] without any temp. Some editors say you should look at it dry. I don't agree. I think you should look at it with whatever you need to make it work. Because otherwise you can discard a lot of material if you're looking at it dry that you may have been able to use." — Director Ridley Scott, interview with Kevin Reynolds, *The Duellists* DVD

CHAPTER 9: VISUAL EFFECTS IN YOUR BLOCKBUSTER

"All art is technology. That's the very nature of it. The artist is always bumping against that technology." — George Lucas, *Cutting Edge: The Magic of Movie Editing* documentary

"If *Jaws* never existed, except in the year 2005, I would have had the digital tools to have had much more of the shark in the movie. Therefore, I would have ruined much more of the movie!" — Steven Spielberg, *The Shark Is Still Working: The Impact and Legacy of Jaws* documentary

CHAPTER 10: MUSIC IN YOUR BLOCKBUSTER

"Music is dialogue." — Ridley Scott, *Breaking the Silence: The Making of Hannibal* DVD

"Ask: What is the emotional undercurrent that the music is playing? And if there's not an answer for that, then there shouldn't be any music." Robert Zemeckis, director's commentary, *Cast Away* DVD

"Very often the music will let the audience know it's okay to think this is ridiculous because the storytellers think this is ridiculous." — John McTiernan, director's commentary, *Die Hard* DVD

CHAPTER 11: SOUND IN YOUR BLOCKBUSTER

"The only way to deal with chaotic battles is to figure out what to lose. 'Cause at the end of the day, if I played everything I had, it would be sonic mud." — Chris Boyes, sound-mixing featurette on *Return of the King* Blu-ray

CHAPTER 12: EXPLOSIVE FINALE — CONCLUSION

"What does the audience want? Well, they don't know what they want. They just know that they want it, and they'll know what that is when they see it." — Christopher Nolan, *Variety*, "Christopher Nolan Gets Candid on the State of Movies, Rise of TV and Spielberg's Influence."

ABOUT THE AUTHOR

Paul Dudbridge is a British director, producer, cinematographer, and educator, making feature films, television, commercials, and music videos.

Paul started producing at the age of 11 when he convinced his father to shoot his first short film. When the resulting footage didn't match up to what he'd seen in his head, Paul went behind the camera himself, igniting his lifelong interest in making films and studying directing, screenwriting, and camerawork.

With over 20 years' experience in the business, Paul has numerous film and television credits to his name. His first broadcast credits include producing and directing ITV's *The Christmas Storybook*, featuring legendary actor Joss Ackland, as well as directing music promos for MTV. His work as a cinematographer includes the action thriller *By Any Name*, based on the bestselling book by Katherine John. As a producer and director, he helmed the science-fiction series *Horizon*, winner of a number of international film festival awards and a nomination for Paul for Best Drama Director at the Royal Television Society (West of England) Awards in 2016.

When not filming, Paul guest-lectures at various universities and colleges around the United Kingdom. Most recently, he ran the

Writing and Directing module for the Master's course at the University of Bristol, taught cinematography at the Falmouth University School of Film & Television, and Advanced Cinematography workshops for BECTU, the United Kingdom's media and entertainment trade union. His first book, *Shooting Better Movies: The Student Filmmakers' Guide*, was released by Michael Wiese Productions in 2017.

When he's not making or watching films, Paul enjoys reading, chess, fitness, and Eastern philosophy. He lives in Bristol, England.

SHOOTING BETTER MOVIES
THE STUDENT FILMMAKERS' GUIDE

PAUL DUDBRIDGE

A one-stop film school, this book is packed with information, tips, techniques, and advice covering all aspects of filmmaking as gathered from the author's years of experience working in short films, features, commercials, and music videos, as well as delivering workshops and lectures to film students of all ages. Everything you need to know — from generating an idea to delivering a finished film — is laid out in an informal and easy-to-read style.

"Nailed it! A simple, turbo-fast read. A practical, no-nonsense, encouraging guide to filmmaking. Students of film, from the initiate to the updating pro, will enrich their knowledge and confidence with Shooting Better Movies. Where was this when I started?"

> — Pen Densham, Oscar-nominated writer, producer, director, Trilogy Entertainment Group principal, *Robin Hood: Prince of Thieves, Backdraft, Moll Flanders, Blown Away, Tank Girl, Outer Limits*

"A valuable resource for anyone starting out on their filmmaking journey."

> — Dr. Neil Fox, Course Coordinator, BA (Hons) Film, Falmouth University, UK

"Dudbridge orchestrates within this do-it-yourself manual a stirring and sustained call to action: while providing a well-structured, informative guide to the essential principles and practice of filmmaking, he never stops emphasizing the importance of learning through the experiences of real-world film production. His passion and persuasiveness are equally infectious. If you are serious about making your student films stand out from their competition, you need to read this book."

> — Stephen Gordon, Senior Lecturer in Film Production Technology, Birmingham City University (UK)

PAUL DUDBRIDGE is a British director, producer, cinematographer, and educator, making feature films, television, commercials, and music videos. His work as a cinematographer includes the action thriller *By Any Name*, based on the bestselling book by Katherine John.

$26.95 · 186 PAGES · ORDER #247RLS · ISBN 9781615932719

FILM DIRECTING: SHOT BY SHOT
VISUALIZING FROM CONCEPT TO SCREEN

25TH ANNIVERSARY EDITION

STEVEN D. KATZ

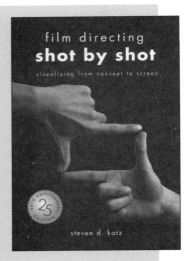

Shot by Shot is the world's go-to directing book, now newly updated for a special 25th Anniversary edition! The first edition sold over 250,000 copies, making it one of the bestselling books on film directing of all time. Aspiring directors, cinematographers, editors, and producers, many of whom are now working professionals, learned the craft of visual storytelling from *Shot by Shot*, the most complete source for preplanning the look of a movie.

The book contains over 800 photos and illustrations, and is by far the most comprehensive look at shot design in print, containing storyboards from movies such as *Citizen Kane*, *Blade Runner*, *Deadpool*, and *Moonrise Kingdom*. Also introduced is the concept of A, I, and L patterns as a way to simplify the hundreds of staging choices facing a director in every scene.

Shot by Shot uniquely blends story analysis with compositional strategies, citing examples then illustrated with the storyboards used for the actual films. Throughout the book, various visual approaches to short scenes are shown, exposing the directing processes of our most celebrated auteurs — including a meticulous, lavishly illustrated analysis of Steven Spielberg's scene design for *Empire of the Sun*.

Overall, the book has new storyboards and concept art, rewritten text for several chapters to address the needs of the YouTube generation of filmmakers, and an enhanced, expanded list of filmmaking resources.
- New introduction
- New storyboards: *Moonrise Kingdom*, *Deadpool*
- Six rewritten chapters detailing new trends and new digital production tools
- New section: Short Cuts
- Visual update: Dozens of illustrations are now shaded to maximize readability
- New bibliography
- New list of online resources

STEVEN D. KATZ is an award-winning writer, producer, and director. His work has appeared on *Saturday Night Live* and in many cable and theatrically released films, such as *Clear and Present Danger*, for which he completed the first full digital previsualization of a motion picture. He has taught workshops at the American Film Institute, Sundance Film Festival, Parsons School of Design, Danish Film Institute, School for Visual Arts (in New York), and Shanghai University, among many others.

$31.95 · 400 PAGES · ISBN 9781615932979

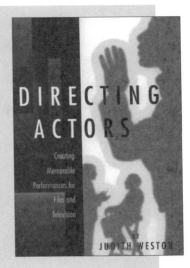

SAVE THE CAT!®
THE LAST BOOK ON SCREENWRITING YOU'LL EVER NEED!

BLAKE SNYDER

BEST SELLER

He's made millions of dollars selling screenplays to Hollywood and now screenwriter Blake Snyder tells all. "Save the Cat!®" is just one of Snyder's many ironclad rules for making your ideas more marketable and your script more satisfying — and saleable, including:

- · The four elements of every winning logline.
- · The seven immutable laws of screenplay physics.
- · The 10 genres and why they're important to your movie.
- · Why your Hero must serve your idea.
- · Mastering the Beats.
- · Mastering the Board to create the Perfect Beast.
- · How to get back on track with ironclad and proven rules for script repair.

This ultimate insider's guide reveals the secrets that none dare admit, told by a show biz veteran who's proven that you can sell your script if you can save the cat.

"Imagine what would happen in a town where more writers approached screenwriting the way Blake suggests? My weekend read would dramatically improve, both in sellable/producible content and in discovering new writers who understand the craft of storytelling and can be hired on assignment for ideas we already have in house."
> – From the Foreword by Sheila Hanahan Taylor, Vice President, Development at Zide/Perry Entertainment, whose films include *American Pie, Cats and Dogs, Final Destination*

"One of the most comprehensive and insightful how-to's out there. Save the Cat!® is a must-read for both the novice and the professional screenwriter."
> – Todd Black, Producer, *The Pursuit of Happyness, The Weather Man, S.W.A.T, Alex and Emma, Antwone Fisher*

"Want to know how to be a successful writer in Hollywood? The answers are here. Blake Snyder has written an insider's book that's informative — and funny, too."
> – David Hoberman, Producer, *The Shaggy Dog* (2005), *Raising Helen, Walking Tall, Bringing Down the House, Monk* (TV)

BLAKE SNYDER, besides selling million-dollar scripts to both Disney and Spielberg, was one of Hollywood's most successful spec screenwriters. Blake's vision continues on *www.blakesnyder.com.*

$20.95 · 216 PAGES · ORDER NUMBER 34RLS · ISBN: 9781932907001

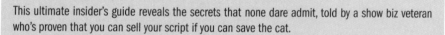

THE *MASTER SHOTS* SERIES

MASTER SHOTS VOL 1 – 2ND EDITION
100 ADVANCED CAMERA TECHNIQUES TO GET AN EXPENSIVE LOOK ON YOUR LOW-BUDGET MOVIE

CHRISTOPHER KENWORTHY

$28.95 · 362 PAGES · ORDER #179RLS · ISBN 9781615930876

MASTER SHOTS VOL 2
100 WAYS TO SHOOT GREAT DIALOGUE SCENES

CHRISTOPHER KENWORTHY

$28.95 · 240 PAGES · ORDER #167RLS · ISBN 9781615930555

MASTER SHOTS VOL 3
THE DIRECTOR'S VISION: 100 SETUPS, SCENES AND MOVES FOR YOUR BREAKTHROUGH MOVIE

CHRISTOPHER KENWORTHY

$28.95 · 238 PAGES · ORDER #196RLS · ISBN 9781615931545

CHRISTOPHER KENWORTHY is the creator of a new series of *Master Shots* e-books (with HD video and audio) including *Master Shots: Action*, *Master Shots: Suspense*, and *Master Shots: Story*. He has worked as a writer, director, and producer for the past thirteen years. He directed *The Sculptor's Ritual*, which played to sold-out screenings in Australia and received strong reviews. Christopher works on music videos, visual effects tutorials, and commercial projects. He's the author of the best-selling *Master Shots Vol 1* and *Master Shots Vol 2*, with *Master Shots Vol 3: The Director's Vision* released in 2013. He's the author of two novels and many short stories. Born in England, he currently lives in Australia with two daughters and the actor Molly Kerr.

JOHN BADHAM ON DIRECTING
NOTES FROM THE SET OF SATURDAY NIGHT FEVER, WARGAMES, *AND MORE*

JOHN BADHAM

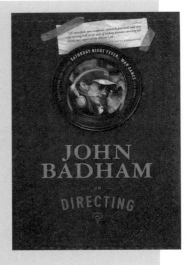

Veteran director John Badham explains the elements of action and suspense and dissects the essentials of any good scene from any genre. Whether you're an actor, director, cinematographer, production designer, or any other creative, Badham gives you the tools to deconstruct and solve scenes.

"I always felt the essence of cinema was the coming together of acting and writing. There are many books on the topics related to directing, but I feel that John Badham's first section on acting is worth its weight in gold. There are many skills involved in making a motion picture, but few so important as working with (and understanding) the actors. That's probably why of all the migrations possible to become a director, few are as successful or plentiful as that of actor to director. This book clearly lays out truthful principles in helping an actor achieve his goals in a way I've never seen before. The other two sections are full of helpful tips as well, but Part 1 is essential for anyone who is serious about directing."
— Francis Coppola

"Ace director John Badham's handbook, John Badham on Directing, is a mercifully non-academic, extremely practical and very entertaining look at the task of making pictures, covering just about every aspect of the director's job. It is not in the least didactic, and includes a multitude of quotes from other filmmakers that are also most illuminating. The book is quite charming as well, and should become a standard text."
— Peter Bogdanovich

"I've been directing for a lot of years, but I wish this book had been around when I first started. It would have made my life a lot easier as a director. One hell of a good read!"
— Richard Donner, Director, Lethal Weapon, Superman, The Omen, Goonies

JOHN BADHAM is the award-winning director of such classic films as *Saturday Night Fever*, *Stake Out*, and *WarGames* and such top TV shows as *Heroes*, *The Shield*, and *Crossing Jordan*. Badham currently is the DeMille Professor of Film and Media at Chapman University.

$26.95 · 240 PAGES · ORDER #197RLS · ISBN 9781615931385

In a dark time, a light bringer came along, leading the curious and the frustrated to clarity and empowerment. It took the well-guarded secrets out of the hands of the few and made them available to all. It spread a spirit of openness and creative freedom, and built a storehouse of knowledge dedicated to the betterment of the arts.

The essence of the Michael Wiese Productions (MWP) is empowering people who have the burning desire to express themselves creatively. We help them realize their dreams by putting the tools in their hands. We demystify the sometimes secretive worlds of screenwriting, directing, acting, producing, film financing, and other media crafts.

By doing so, we hope to bring forth a realization of 'conscious media' which we define as being positively charged, emphasizing hope and affirming positive values like trust, cooperation, self-empowerment, freedom, and love. Grounded in the deep roots of myth, it aims to be healing both for those who make the art and those who encounter it. It hopes to be transformative for people, opening doors to new possibilities and pulling back veils to reveal hidden worlds.

MWP has built a storehouse of knowledge unequaled in the world, for no other publisher has so many titles on the media arts. Please visit www.mwp.com where you will find many free resources and a 25% discount on our books. Sign up and become part of the wider creative community!

Onward and upward,

Michael Wiese
Publisher/Filmmaker